D0871625

THE KEY TO PEACE

by

CLARENCE MANION

A formula for the perpetuation of real Americanism

1951

The Heritage Foundation, Inc.

75 EAST WACKER DRIVE

CHICAGO 1, ILL.

AN APPRAISAL

THE AUTHOR emphasizes that our free institutions rest upon the religious conviction that every individual is a child of God and therefore is of supreme worth.

It is to be hoped that this book will be read by leaders of opinion, by students, and indeed by every thoughtful person who wants to help preserve the American form of Government.

Dean Manion's book gives the one certain method for making freedom strong in our time. It is one of the greatest books of all my reading experience and I commend it to every patriotic man and woman.

NORMAN VINCENT PEALE

FOREWORD

Deep-planted in the consciousness of the peoples of the world is remembrance of the toil, the tears, the blood and the incredible destructions of two world wars. With mounting alarm we sense the prospect of yet another world-wide holocaust which well may bring a terror and a devastation the like of which has not yet been imagined.

Into this surcharged atmosphere one of America's great scholars has injected a reconsideration of fundamental proposals that hold the Key to Peace. To the subject he contributes a genius for simplification that clarifies a truth which a generation of scholarship has shrouded with complications and obscurities.

The author demonstrates that the one and only possible formula for peace was discovered by the Founding Fathers when they indited and implemented the American Declaration of Independence. When the formula was established in the American constitutional system a miracle resulted.

> "The whole atmosphere of the United States seemed charged with a kind of electricity that sparked the human spirit in a manner that was beyond all earthly precedent."

By traveling this road peace can be attained and preserved. The road is as clearly marked as a six lane superhighway. The procedure proposed is as simple as a little red school house blackboard problem in primer arithmetic. Nevertheless, simple as it is, the formula has its price. The author states that—

> "a bloody Revolution was necessary to establish it. A desperate Civil War was necessary to maintain it. May God grant that the time may never come, but, if it becomes essential, other wars must be fought to preserve and perpetuate this exclusive and priceless heritage, for it is—the Key to Peace."

To most readers the author will need no introduction. However, for more than a quarter of a century Clarence Manion has been one of America's most noted professors of Constitutional Law. He is the distinguished Dean of the College of Law of Notre Dame University, the founder and the builder of the Natural Law Institute. He is a recognized writer of meaningful prose and a popular lecturer of unusual persuasiveness. For his outstanding writings and addresses on Americanism he was voted the Freedom Award in 1950.

With an insight that approaches the prophetic, Dean Manion seems to sense the unsatisfied yearnings, the distrusts and the frustrations of modern Americans. His appraisal of the causes of the restlessness and the confusion of our times is original and unique. The mountain of evidence he provides as to the ordained purpose of this nation is startling. His explanation of the fundamental differences between the French and the American Revolutions is enlightening. His contention that the ownership of property is a duty and an obligation rather than a right, and that there need be no limit to property accumulations, is both refreshing and convincing. No one has so clearly and graphically defined the irreconcilable differences and distinctions between the American concept and Communism — the final flowering of Socialistic theory and practice.

The evidence that is presented and the dramatic story that is told might have been the life-time work of a clergyman of any religious denomination. However, Dean Manion is a layman. The case that is made automatically applies to all who seek Divine guidance, but it should have special point and meaning for that tragic fringe of agnostics who acknowledge no allegiance or who give merely lip service to organized religious institutions.

The publication of this book would have been more than justified for the exclusive purpose of re-emphasizing the relatively unknown but truly vital decision of the United States Supreme Court in 1892 and the excerpts from the Preambles of forty-seven State Constitutions. These are found in the appendix. Mr. Manion has given substance and meaning and life to these all but forgotten statements of basic purpose.

Dean Clarence Manion has written into this unusual and remarkable document a thrilling message of hope. May you who read it be inspired to rededicate your lives to the perpetuation of real Americanism, for in real Americanism, as the author proves, lies the last best hope of "peace on earth". J.M.P.

THE PUBLISHERS

Table of Contents

●

PROLOGUE

Mᴏʀᴇ ᴛʜᴀɴ ꜰɪꜰᴛʏ ʏᴇᴀʀꜱ ᴀɢᴏ, the Reverend Russell Conwell of Philadelphia delivered more than five thousand times a lecture which was titled "Acres of Diamonds."

The lecture was built around the fabulous story of a Persian farmer named Hafed. To Hafed's home one day came a mystical wise man of the East who fascinated the farmer with a long and thrilling story about the value and beauty of diamonds. With a handful of diamonds, the visitor explained, Hafed could buy the whole county and with a diamond mine he would be rich enough to rule the world.

The eloquent visitor assured Hafed that great quantities of diamonds were located in various parts of the world merely waiting to be discovered—all one had to do was to find them. Hafed was enchanted. He forthwith sold his farm and sallied forth visiting many far away countries in his search. He found no diamonds.

Years later, long after the weary and penniless Hafed had died tragically in a strange land, another Persian while digging in Hafed's deserted garden discovered the diamond mines of Golconda, the richest ever uncovered in the ancient world.

Confusion In Our Times

THE UNITED STATES is searching for the wealth of peace and prosperity that lies in a solution of extremely practical problems. As we march into the depressing maze of controversy over strikes, wages, profits, prices, production and the threat of war we feel the white heat of atomic energy on our heels. Will all our accumulations be reduced to rubble in a forthcoming atomic conflict? We know that unless we can simultaneously find a solution called permanent international peace, all the rest of our discoveries will go for naught. In the frenzy of our search we are willing to go anywhere and do anything but to date—like Hafed—we have shown little interest in the possibilities of our own back yard.

The men of George Washington's generation had no opportunity to view the sweeping landscapes of America from a speeding airplane or to make a half dozen routine trips from coast to coast within the span of a single calendar year. They missed the majestic perspective of peak and prairie that comprise "America the Beautiful," but in the faces of their fellow countrymen they saw something far more important, something which our contemporaries have missed entirely. The widely diversified population of Revolutionary America reflected a fleeting vision of eternal truth-in-action which our alert and farsighted forefathers caught on the wing.

CONFLICTING INTERESTS For practical purposes the Americans of 1776 had little in common except a common faith and a common enemy. Throughout the American colonies at that time were widely separated groups of people speaking many languages and cherishing widely different ancestral traditions. Less than a third of the population was of English descent. The balance was largely Dutch, Irish, German, Swedish, Scotch, French, Italian, Portuguese and Moravian. At that time all of these people were united in the fight against England, but they were far from reconciled to each other. The English portion of the population itself was split into many self-conscious groups, such as Puritans, Cavaliers, Catholics and Quakers. An important consideration in the selection of George Washington as commander-in-chief of the American Army was the necessity for convincing the English of New England that the Cavaliers of Virginia were seriously and permanently in the War for Independence.

That war-time generation—like our own—was in mortal terror of a "separate peace." Like ourselves, they too worried about what would happen when the enemy was finally defeated and the common danger thus suddenly withdrawn. We have seen the effect upon our so recently solid union of "gallant devoted allies" once the diabolical presence of Hitler was removed from the scene. Should the wartime union of American Colonies and Colonists be as speedily dissolved once the Revolutionary War was won? The most distinguished "Foreign Commentators" of that day flatly predicted that this disruption would certainly take place. They assumed that the disintegrating influences of race, religion, language and geography would immediately split the so-called "United" states asunder.

INTERNAL STRIFE Soon after the last British army had surrendered, events began to shape up just as the "experts" had predicted. The "groups," "divisions" and "classes" of the American population began to move against one another. Conflicts and disagreements between regions, races, farmers, merchants, debtors, creditors, soldiers and civilians flared up violently in all parts of the country. Nevertheless the warring *factions* and *classes* were never quite able to close their respective ranks. The groups failed to "jell." Some indescribable, but nevertheless persistent and effective influence was everywhere at work dissolving the solidarity of opposing factions. The expected disintegration of the American people into little warring islands of Quakers, Puritans, Germans, French, Swedes, Irish, English, Farmers, Merchants, and others threatened seriously but never quite materialized.

MAGIC INGREDIENT Gradually it became evident that in and by the American Revolution the United States had achieved something far more important than mere independence. The Revolution had brought forth and moved into action on this continent, and for the first time in Human History, a genuine cure for the social cancer of class-consciousness and group antagonism.

The American Revolution had produced a workable common denominator for people of many races, many creeds and widely separated economic circumstances. Through this magical and mysterious force the American Union slowly but surely became "more perfect."

It was soon evident that this unique American formula was no mere temporary makeshift. On the contrary it quickly developed dynamic qualities and magnetic influences that spread abroad and tugged at the hearts of men all over the world. Great waves of immigration surged toward the new and rapidly expanding United States. The sharp diversities of the American Revolutionary population were multiplied ten thousand times in hundreds of American communities that spread steadily from coast to coast.

In all of these places the strange new American formula went quickly and quietly to work. Group solidarities were disintegrated and murderous class-consciousness, then as now the scourge of the Old World, was quickly dissolved. At the same time the downtrodden failures of other countries found new and successful personal lives in the United States.

VAST IMMIGRATION In the year 1921 Congress placed drastic restrictions upon all immigration to the United States. Then, and not until then, the great torrential influx of foreigners slowed down to a mere trickle. In one hundred and thirty years approximately 40 million immigrants entered the United States and were chiefly responsible for increasing our population from four million in 1790 to one hundred and eight million in 1921. This was "the most remarkable peaceful mass movement of population in all history."

It is, to say the least, "remarkable" that continuously for more than one hundred and thirty years, millions of people were leaving each and all of the countries of Europe to find a common home in a place called the United States of America.

Throughout this entire period there were countries other than the United States where the climate was as good or better, where fertile land was even more plentiful and where there were (and still are) fewer people per square mile of territory. Nevertheless, the immigrants insisted upon coming here and come they did in ever-increasing numbers until Congress closed the gate.

A person's decision to emigrate is sharp on both sides. He is dissatisfied where he is and he is attracted to the place where he is going. Our immigration statistics reveal a widespread and continuous state of dissatisfaction with living conditions and opportunities in all European countries between 1790 and 1921. They likewise show a striking unanimity of opinion as to the place where living conditions and opportunities were good enough to justify the great effort and sacrifice entailed in pulling up stakes and going there. Tens of millions of people in all civilized nations have made and acted upon this difficult decision against their own countries and in favor of ours.

What does this prove? It proves first of all that the political and economic system of Europe is now and has always been radically different from the political and economic system of the United States. It proves that in the estimation of Europeans themselves the American system is incomparably superior to that of Europe. It proves finally that we as citizens and residents of the United States exercise one of the highest and most closely held privileges obtainable in this world.

BEGINNINGS AND ACCOMPLISHMENT Of the millions who emigrated to this country between the Presidencies of Washington and Wilson, all but a few began their life here as manual laborers. With pitchfork and pruning-shears, hammer and hoe, pick and power-tool these "peaceful movers" helped to push our industrial frontiers into rich fields of new opportunity for themselves and those who were to follow.

It is true that the newcomers were not always welcomed by those who had arrived here a few generations ahead of them. At succeeding and recurring intervals the immigrants were sure to be pitied, despised, ostracized and "exploited." They worked long, hard hours before blazing furnaces or in steaming swamps, or badly ventilated factories. By our present standards their wages were pitifully small but compared to conditions then prevailing in Europe their life and work in America appeared as an undisguised blessing to them. Much of their savings went back across the sea to supplement the meager living standards of loved ones necessarily left behind.

Eventually, many of the new Americans were financially able to bring these fathers, brothers, uncles and cousins over here to share the land of freedom, opportunity and enterprise.

Today, the names of these immigrants and those of their descendants lead all the rest on our lists of savings bank depositors, home owners, and common corporate stockholders. Thus has activated Americanism enabled millions of people to emerge from the hopelessness of European drudgery, enjoy freedom and earn economic independence.

SOMETHING REALLY NEW Few of these grateful immigrants ever probed the mystery of their transformation but they never ceased to wonder at it. True enough, the lands, lakes, mountains and rivers of the New World were not unlike those of the Old, yet the whole atmosphere of the United States seemed charged with a kind of electricity that sparked the human spirit in a manner that was beyond all earthly precedent. Feuds

that had tortured the long history of the European home-
lands failed to take permanent roots in the soil of America.
Thus in the new American spirit of concert and concord,
all the people of the earth contributed to a miraculously
quick and magnificent development of the greatest civilization that the world has ever seen.

Through many successive generations the advantages
and achievements of our country were abundantly multiplied. Then, as its benefits developed into routine, the
enticing mystery of American life ceased to challenge the
interest of its beneficiaries. The American system came to
be taken for granted. All were satisfied in the conviction
that here was the promised land; that here, as in no other
country on earth, the human spirit inevitably found satis-
fying refuge. Few really knew what it was that made
America "tick"—but until our very own time all were
agreed that the genuine and really precious diamonds of
human civilization were to be found only in this—the
United States of America.

**TRAGEDY OF
ACHIEVEMENT**
Today, this traditional American confidence has disappeared. America and
Americans have suddenly ceased to be
different from other countries and other peoples. We have
caught the world-wide contagion of doubt and with doubt
has come discord. The good earth of American unity now
quakes repeatedly. Wide chasms appear to separate the
"classes," the "races" and other self-conscious "groups" of
people who now make up the present population of the

United States. Across their respective ramparts these suddenly segmented areas of our citizenship shout at one another in the time-honored old-world fashion, using the time-honored old-world phraseology. We set out to bridge the new chasms with "inter-faith" and "inter-race" and "inter-class" movements, all of which carry on their faces an open admission that the mysterious magnetic unity of all-American men and women is in eclipse. Instead of that traditional unity we now propose that "Labor" shall make a "truce" or a "treaty" with "Capital"; that the "Gentiles" shall be *tolerant* of the "Jews" and that the "Special Privileged," the "Underprivileged," the "Haves" and the "Have Nots" shall be permanently walled away from each other by the sharp barrier of a new "Social Consciousness."

ONE WORLD The old cocksure confidence in the manifest destiny of American principle to save mankind has given way to fear and frustration. We are now in the process of considering the proposal that the "one world forced upon us by the Atom bomb shall be the *Old* World rather than the *New*. To the ailing and discouraged spirit of mankind we no longer offer a panacea. The traditional pride in America and the traditional confidence in the potency of American principle are now dissolved in a multitude of more "modern" more "realistic" solutions produced in foreign countries where the people would give anything they possess in exchange for an opportunity to live in the United States.

Strange as it may seem, our envious enemies abroad are now joined by powerful and influential "intellectuals" of the United States in a concerted drive to discredit the American heritage. At the same time the "Experts," like Hafed, take off for the Mountains of the Moon in search of ways and means to pacify and unify mankind.

Nevertheless, the historical fact remains that the matchless American formula for unity-in-freedom carries the best of all obtainable recommendations, namely, that *it has worked*. It has worked because it is right.

Two Revolutions

A SOCIAL AND POLITICAL system is the product of the events of its underlying history in the same way that a ripe tomato is the product of its seed and soil. Other things being equal, the quantity of manganese in a particular piece of ground will determine the size, quality and texture of the tomatoes we plant there. In like manner, when the two systems of society mature in the same period of time with radically opposite characteristics we may be sure that important differences exist in the soil of their respective histories. This is undoubtedly true of the institutions known respectively as Americanism and Europeanism. Since the Social Scientists have refused or neglected to do so, let us make parallel analyses of the historical top-soil from which these two institutions emanate and carefully note their respective ingredients.

SIMILARITIES AND DIFFERENCES Our examination discloses certain elements common to both systems. Each was the formal and deliberate product of revolutionary action taken in the last quarter of the 18th Century. Americanism proceeded directly from the American Revolution of 1776; Europeanism from the French Revolution of 1789. Both revolutions involved substantially the same races of people. Certain resemblances are likewise observable in the unofficial vocabularies of each movement. At this point the similarities cease and important differences appear.

The most striking and significant differences are found in the respective directions of the two revolutions and in the type of force generated by each of them. The French Revolution turned in the direction of the glorified—even deified—"Society" or "State." It generated a centrifugal force which tore apart and disintegrated the individual human personality, the natural hub of all social order and flung its fragments out to the rim where the broken pieces were congealed in the form of social and economic "classes." Thereafter, the European "citizen" ceased to be a man and became instead a part of the "proletariat," the "aristocracy" or the "bourgeoisie." In this manner the individual European lost his intrinsic importance. His personality was drowned in his "class" and in order to survive, he was forced to become and remain acutely "class-conscious."

The French Revolutionary State did not recognize its citizens or subjects as men. Individuals, as such, had no rights that this strange new government was bound to respect. The basic fact that each person is an indestructible creature of God was categorically and officially denied.

**FRENCHMEN
DELUDED**
Nevertheless, the Paris Mob which battered down the doors of the Bastille in 1789 firmly believed that universal "liberty, equality and fraternity" would be the reward of their glorious "democratic" revolution. To these frenzied and frustrated men the accursed and hated despotism was necessarily personified under the crown of the King. With this fixation the rabid and roaring crowd was highly conditioned and thoroughly malleable material for the Socialistic leaders of the revolution who were determined merely to displace the time-honored tyranny of the reigning monarch with the new and more ruthless tyranny of "the Masses." These Socialistic leaders "sold" the mob on the idea that "no man should continue to give himself to another man called a King, but where the *authority* of *all* is established over *each,* each thus gives himself to none." Upon this specious pretext the dictatorship of Kings was thereafter supplanted by the Dictatorship of "Society."

Under the new Authoritarian system "Liberty, Equality and Fraternity" quickly faded into a hypocritical figure of speech. Liberty was discarded the minute the authority of God, the Author of liberty, was denied. Thereafter the State was supreme and its subjects consequently had no rights beyond those which the State chose to concede.

**EQUALITY
vs.
JUSTICE**
The only possible justification for human "Equality" in any sense of the term disappeared in the athiestical materialism of the

French Revolutionary State. In a physical and material sense all men are naturally *unequal*. Look over any large or small company of men and women anywhere in the world—Do you observe a community of "equal" human beings? Have you ever found any two people in the whole world—now or in history—who at any time in their lives were equally wise, handsome, powerful or resourceful, and equal in all of these qualities at one and the same time? It is immediately obvious that these attributes are always distributed with persistent inequality amongst all individual persons throughout the world. Then what becomes of that "self-evident" truth about the equality of all men that is mentioned in our American Declaration of Independence?

It must be observed that the Declaration states that "all men are *created* equal." This is indeed a very special kind of equality. It is deliberately related to the Creator and signifies that in their "divine" endowments and in their divinely ordained purpose, men are all the same. Thus the life of any man is just as sacred as the life of any other, and each man has exactly the same natural rights and duties as every other person. All persons have a common origin and a common end. Before their common Creator each has equally great importance. Being thus equal before God, they must likewise be equal before the Constitutions and laws of the land.

This Equality before their Creator neither contemplates nor calls for a dead level in the earthly condition of men. On the contrary each human being is by nature a distinct individual personality and is consequently and naturally different in his earthly characteristics from every other person on earth. The confusion of "inequality" with "injustice" is a fatal mistake which frustrates many well-intentioned attempts to improve human society. Injustice is vicious and must be fought unceasingly, but inequality is a natural and inescapable characteristic of the human race.

VARIETY AND PROGRESS There has never been nor will there ever be a time when all men are equal in their capacities and conditions here on earth. The nature of the individual as well as the nature and continuity of human society, demands these unfailing differences. Without the wide diversification of talents, taste, abilities and ambitions that now and always exist among men, Society could neither feed nor clothe itself. It is consequently a wise provision of Providence that causes the perpetuation of endless variety in the desires and capabilities of human beings. Sparked with personal liberty and the natural personal incentive to own property and advance economically this conglomeration of inequality synchronizes into a great engine for the sustenance and progress of mankind.

MATERIALISTIC RESULT The French Revolutionary promise of "Fraternity" like its companion-pieces of "liberty," and "equality"—was lost in the materialistic deification of "the State." Fraternity, or brotherhood, results when men have a common Father.

The brotherhood of man consequently proceeds from the common Fatherhood of all men in God, the Creator.

In a materialistic Society which denies the existence and authority of God, the appeal for human brotherhood is a curious contradiction in terms. The battle-cry of the French Revolution for "liberty, equality and fraternity" was thus shrewd but none-the-less deliberate demigogery on part of its Socialist leaders. The slogan was calculated merely to capitalize upon the misery of the poor and set them apart as "a class" against the hated "Aristocracy."

In the ensuing terror of the class warfare which these Revolutionary leaders generated, "Liberty, Equality and Fraternity" were conspicuous by their complete absence.

OPPORTUNITY FOR OPPORTUNISTS   Our analysis of the French Revolutionary System discloses class-conscious collectivism as its controlling ingredient. From the philosophers and first leaders of the French Revolution, Rousseau, Danton, Robiespierre and others, this collectivist formula was passed to and used by succeeding European opportunists. Napoleon, Mussolini and Hitler each whipped it into a potent and destructive doctrine of racism. Karl Marx and his disciples including Lenin, Trotsky and Stalin gave class-conscious collectivism an economic fluidity which spilled it over all geographical and racial barriers with the potentiality of flooding the entire world. Quickly, and in one form or another, French Revolutionary collectivism spread yet another layer of Statism all over

Europe. Wherever it went it promptly split the basic natural atom of Human Society—the individual human soul—and in so doing, shook the whole unhappy continent with continual catastrophic explosions of panic, pestilence and persecution.

THE AMERICAN SYSTEM Meanwhile, on the other side of the world we find our own Revolution spinning in the exactly opposite direction. The American Revolution turned directly away from collectivism and toward the basic integrity of the individual man. In so doing it generated a centripetal force which destroyed class-consciousness in the diversified groups of our Revolutionary population. This centripetal force was definitely integrating in its quality and effects. It pulled out of each group the individual God-created human soul and anchored it in the core and center of our social order as the vital pivot of the American political system.

Our forefathers were wise enough to see that this indestructible soul was the eternal quality that all Americans —indeed that all men everywhere—had and have in common with one another. Far from making a new God out of "Society" the American Revolution was an official public acknowledgment of the one true pre-existing God, the Creator of all men and source of all the rights of men. While the Europeans were sowing the materialistic winds of their political and economic storms, our Founding Fathers were building Americanism upon the firm foundations of religious faith. When the French Revolutionaries were hammering men into mere matter, the American Revolutionaries were exalting and safeguarding man's spirit. The European system was moulding men into "masses" and "classes" at the same time that the American system was dedicating itself to the task of preserving the integrity of the "individual Personality."

DEATHLESS DECLARATION So that there could be no possible mistake about its object and purpose, our Founding Fathers caused the American Republic officially and with the first breath of its new life to declare:

> "We hold these truths to be self-evident; that all men are created equal; that they are endowed by their Creator with certain unalienable rights; that among these are life, liberty and the pursuit of happiness. That to secure these rights, governments are instituted among men, deriving their just powers from the consent of the governed—"

Here is the distilled essence of Americanism as stated in the first official document of the new United States of America, the Declaration of Independence. These are the eternal principles upon which our Puritans, Cavaliers, Catholics, Protestants, Jews, Gentiles, French, Germans, Dutch, Swedes, Scotch, Irish and others came together on a permanent and peaceful basis. Because each of them was equal before God, all of these people were made equal before the law of the land. Because their rights were bestowed by their Heavenly Creator, no power on *earth* could take those rights away. Since God had created each of them as individuals with personal and immortal destinies, no man, majority or government could hereafter treat or regard any of them as an indistinguishable part of a class, collective or group.

REVOLUTION STILL WORKING These are the basic articles of our American Faith. They constitute the axes upon which the wheels of our dynamic American Revolution go round and round even to this hour. In other parts of the world the wheels of materialistic skepticism still whirl in the opposite direction. The two revolutionary forces are violently opposed to one another. Each tends to draw first into its orbit and then into its vortex all political, economic and social movements as rapidly as they appear in any part of the world. At this time their fight for world supremacy is more bitter than ever before, and there is universal consciousness of the fact that one or the other of these two forces eventually must triumph.

SUICIDAL ENTRAPMENT In America today the grinding noise of the turning European wheel is ever more and more audible. Sparks from its materialistic engine fall constantly on all parts of the United States. Here on our very own soil fanatical firebrands of Europeanism are constantly directing these sparks to the more inflammable portions of our American social order; to "minority groups" to "labor," to "capital," to "consumers," and to "producers" to the "little fellows," to the "special interests," to the "haves" and to the "have nots."

In our confusion we give the firebrands an initial and partial success by fighting back with their own choice of weapons, namely, "class consciousness." We let them skillfully trap us into a defense of or an attack upon these "classes" as such, instead of striking at the firebrands themselves with the sharp and devastating weapon forged in our own Revolution and unsheathed before the world in the American Declaration of Independence. That weapon is

> the *personal God-given integrity of each free man in the American classless society.*

Not because he is a Jew, Gentile, white, black, consumer, producer, farmer, merchant, laborer or capitalist, but because he is a *man* with a personal immortal destiny, each of our citizens is entitled to the equal protection of American government and to the equal respect of his fellow Americans. Constant reiteration of this basic American doctrine frustrates the disintegrating centrifugal forces of Europeanism by a positive acceleration of our own centripetal machine. No informed American needs to concede anything to any one of the many insidious forms of European Collectivism. Any such concession reverses the unanimous verdict of all of our ancestors.

FOUNDERS FARSIGHTED History shows that in all its forms Collectivism corrodes the nature of men at the same time that it poisons the whole stream of civilization. It is a fanatical and futile effort to substitute a man-made concept for the God-made man.

In their own time our shrewd revolutionary forefathers saw this basic issue of personal rights as clearly as the regulated and regimented Englishman undoubtedly sees it today. The United States was consequently born of the conviction that human rights are worth their price. For the basic all-important natural *right of the individual person against his own government* it was necessary in 1776 to pay the high price of a bloody revolution.

> It so happens that in making this purchase we incidentally cornered the world market on those same rights of the individual against his government, which now and always constitute the sole and only insurance against despotism.

NO COMPE-TITION With one or two highly debatable exceptions, ours is the only country in the whole world in which the individual man holds substantial, natural personal rights he can require everybody, including his government, to respect and observe. This is the goal for which the Founding Fathers risked their "lives," their "fortunes" and their "sacred honor" in their fateful and deathless Declaration of Independence. To attain the great objective it was necessary for them to by-pass contemporary corruption of English constitutional law and drive straight through Magna Charta all the way back to the book of Genesis:

> "And God created man in his own image, Male and Female, He created them."

Many of our American conditions and institutions are a great deal less than perfect. There are inequities and injustices in our country that we can and must remedy. But there is nothing wrong in the United States that any Europeanism can correct or that a firm and fearless application of the principles of our Declaration of Independence cannot cure.

DEMONSTRATED EFFECTIVENESS   All of the foregoing is mere conclusion of fact. Available statistics simply demonstrate that Europe is now and has long been basically deficient in what it takes to contain a large and diversified population in reasonable contentment. Figures likewise show that America has been a magnet for all kinds of people of every race and circumstance and that the same force that drew them here, managed to hold them together in peace and order after they got here. But we must quickly know more than this if we are to preserve this magnetic ingredient of the American System and at the same time, prevent the utter collapse of European civilization.

Why does the American system succeed where the European system fails? If we can answer this question scientifically without rhapsodical guess work, we can save and improve our famed "way of life" and at the same time regenerate the civilization of Europe with a sustained transfusion of basic American principles.

Morality and Faith

OUR AMERICAN forefathers knew that God must be in the government of any people in order to insure them against despotism. This shrewd and practical formula for the protection of human liberty became an integral part of the American political tradition. In that tradition liberty is always honored as a soft, sweet breath of Heaven, just as every form of despotism is despised as a blast from Hell. For 300 years after America was discovered, many varieties of people came here in search of personal liberty. All of them were scrupulous in their official reliance upon God as the source and stem of that precious objective.

GOD GIVEN RIGHTS This official conjunction of the laws of God with the Constitutions and laws of the land is the basic and controlling ingredient of Americanism. Our uniformed policemen— and we use him here as a convenient representative of the whole structure of our state and federal government— merely pokes his club into that calloused and comparatively small area of humanity which the moral law does not penetrate. The uniformed policeman does not originate right and wrong. He merely extends and reinforces the observance of those rights and duties that stem from the Ten Commandments. In all respects he is a mere projection of the individual human conscience and in no case can he be made to substitute for it. On the contrary, a widened sense of individual conscientious responsibility can be made to shorten the policeman's "beat" considerably. It is in this direction—the direction of a more acutely developed sense of individual conscientious responsibility—that we must constantly look for any permanent improvement in the ordered general welfare of our society.

MAN TO MAN JUSTICE It must be remembered that ninety-five percent of the peace, order and welfare existing in human society is always produced by the conscientious practice of man to man justice and person to person charity. When any part of this important domain of personal virtue is transferred to government, that part is automatically released from the restraints of morality and put into the area of conscience-less coercion. The field of personal responsibility is thus reduced at the same time and to the same extent that the boundaries of irresponsibility are enlarged. Expansion of the governmental domain in this manner is unfortunate for two reasons. The first is purely practical: Government cannot manage these fields of human welfare with the justice, economy and effectiveness that is possible when these same fields are the direct responsibility of morally sensitive human beings. This loss of justice, economy and effectiveness is increased in the proportion that such governmental management is centralized. The second reason is basic: Any shrinkage in the area of personal responsibility tends to frustrate the purpose for which man was created. Man is here to be tested for his free compliance with the moral law of God. A great part of this law concerns man's relationships with man.

INDIVIDUAL RESPONSIBILITY Every human being has a God-imposed personal obligation to assist his neighbor when the latter is in poverty, destitution or distress. The government cannot excuse any man from this obligation and it should not pretend to do so. More and more people now shirk this moral duty because they are encouraged to believe that every type of human misery is the exclusive concern of the government. It was the murderer Cain, who first declared that he was not his brother's keeper and for this he has lived in infamy for thousands of years.

MORAL OBLIGATIONS Government cannot make men good; neither can it make them prosperous and happy. The evils in society are directly traceable to the vices of individual human beings. At its best government may simply attack the secondary manifestations of these vices. Their primary manifestations are found in the pride, covetousness, lust, envy, sloth and plain incompetency of individual people. When government goes far beyond this simple duty and deploys its forces along a broad complicated front, under a unified command, it invariably propagates the very evils that it is designed to reduce.

In the sweet name of "human welfare" such a government begins to do things that would be gravely offensive if done by individual citizens. The government is urged to follow this course by people who consciously or subconsciously seek an impersonal outlet for the "primaries" of human weakness. An outlet in other words which will enable them to escape the moral responsibility that would be involved in their personal commission of these sins. As a convenience to this popular attitude we are assured that "government should do for the people what the people are unable to do for themselves." This is an extremely dangerous definition of the purpose of government. It is radically different from the purpose stated in the Declaration of Independence; nevertheless it is now widely accepted as correct.

PETER TO PAY PAUL Here is one example of centralized governmental operation: Paul wants some of Peter's property. For moral as well as legal reasons, Paul is unable personally to accomplish this desire. Paul therefore persuades the government to tax Peter in order to provide funds with which the government pays Paul a "subsidy." Paul now has what he wanted. His conscience is clear and he has proceeded "according to law." Who could ask for more?—why, Paul, of course, and at the very next opportunity. There is nothing to stop him now *except the eventual exhaustion of Peter's resources.*

QUALMS OF CONSCIENCE The fact that there are millions of Pauls and Peters involved in such transactions does not change their essential and common characteristic. The Pauls have simply engaged the government "to do for them (the people) that which they are unable to do for themselves." Had the Pauls done this individually and directly without the help of the government, each of them would have been subject to fine and imprisonment. Furthermore, ninety-five per cent of the Pauls would have refused to do this job because the moral conscience of each Paul would have hurt him if he did. However, where government does it for them, there is no prosecution and no pain in anybody's conscience. This encourages the unfortunate impression that by using the ballot instead of a blackjack we may take whatever we please to take from our neighbors store of rights and immunities.

Big centralized government generates a system of moral anarchy for many of man's common relationships with man. In this manner the growth and centralization of governmental power gradually destroys that sense of individual conscientious responsibility which, as we have seen, is the mainspring of our general welfare. A "Welfare State" is thus a contradiction in terms.

The ultimate good of all humanity can be accomplished only by the advancement of virtue in individual persons. Whereas a community of saints would require no policeman at all, no amount of "government" would be able to produce the general welfare of a community composed of people entirely without morals. Since it is thus impossible to divorce the evils of society from the sins of its individual members, we must consequently develop the general good not from "Statute to Statute" but from "person to person." All of our preachments in promotion of group morality and community welfare will be ineffective so long as they are not accompanied by an improvement in personal morals.

FOUNDERS' FAITH There is nothing new in any of the foregoing conclusions. As we have seen, all the founders of America knew them very well indeed. Like everything else on earth Government is the servant of Almighty God. Blind worship of the servant while the master is ignored is a fatal corruption of both servant and worshipper. Without the supporting sanction of morality no act of government is any stronger than the physical force behind it. In such a situation "might" becomes the sole measure of "right." What gives value, point, permanence and universality to such things as "justice," "human rights," "human liberty," "law" and "order"

> is the ultimate eternal life of each man as conceived by God at the time of creation.

No combination of all the purely material forces on earth can completely and adequately protect your normal and natural "pursuit of happiness." To sustain that pursuit, and all that it implies, "religion and morality are indispensable."

BITTER PILL FOR REFORMERS This is a bitter medicine for the materialistic social reformer who is honestly convinced that justice in general and social justice in particular is the creature of statutes and the end product of professional governmental administration. These materialists have forgotten that in Americanism, justice is a moral concept and that, consequently, all injustice is sinful and evil. We cannot smother this evil with an avalanche of legislation any more than we can perpetuate virtue by embalming it in a well-worded statute. There is no such thing as the mass production of morals, and by the same token we can never produce any kind of justice on a legislative assembly line. To date, nobody has come forward with a *working* formula by which we can make a good society out of bad men. The recent tendency to rely upon such formulas only seems to make our society worse. A social consciousness never can be an effective substitute for the individual conscience.

The Founding Fathers of America accepted no political formula that was not achieved through Divine Guidance.

Their faith in God's providence was unshakeable. George Washington summarized their attitude in his farewell address when he said:

> "Of all the dispositions and habits which lead to political prosperity religion and morality are indispensable supports. Reason and experience both forbid us to expect that natural morality can prevail in exclusion of Religious Principles."

This is the spirit in which American Constitutions were made.

FIRST WRITTEN CONSTITUTION   Probably the first constitution for the complete self-government of the people under its jurisdiction was made in America in the year 1620. It is called "the Mayflower Compact" and it consists of little more than a solemn and simple affirmation of the Moral Law. At that time the little ship "Mayflower" was anchored off the coast of what is now Massachusetts. The ship was there by accident and without official sanction. By the terms of their Commission from the King of England the occupants of the Mayflower should have gone to Virginia. But their energies were exhausted and many of the ship's company were restless and impatient. Under these circumstances the leaders decided to make a landing and a settlement upon the adjacent rocky shore. All understood that when that happened they would become a completely revolutionary community. To buttress themselves against the viscissitudes of anarchy, and while all were still on board, they drew up a "constitution" which all adult members of the company were asked to sign.

From a purely technical standpoint this "constitution" left much to be desired. Among other things it failed to establish either a legislature, an executive or a judiciary, but its opening sentence "In the name of God, Amen" told the whole story. The signers solemnly covenanted:

> "In the presence of God and one another" to combine themselves together "for the preservation and furtherance of the Glory of God and the advancement of the Christian religion."

In their ignorance of technicalities, they were still wise enough to know that a conscientious and universal observance of God's law would insure the peace and tranquility of that or any other community. The History of the Mayflower colony shows that their confidence was not misplaced.

SUPPLEMENTAL RECORD   More than 200 years after the Mayflower Compact (1852), the Indiana Constitutional Convention reiterated the traditional American confidence and trust in the Moral Law with the opening sentence of the present Indiana Constitution:

> "To the end that justice be established, public order maintained and liberty perpetuated; We the People of the State of Indiana, *grateful to Almighty God for the free exercise of the right to choose our own form of government,* do ordain this constitution. We declare that all men are *created* equal; that they are

endowed by their Creator with certain unalienable
rights; that among these are life, liberty and the
pursuit of happiness."

Similar expressions are in the Constitution of *every State
in the Union* except one.*

In this, the American tradition of law and order, a
mere "democratic" or "constitutional form" of government is not enough. Constitutions and Bills of Rights are
but vain and futile barricades against tyranny unless, as
our Declaration of Independence says,

> they are firmly founded in and upon "the laws of
> Nature and of Nature's God."

ORIGIN OF THE FORM The famous Virginia Bill of Rights of 1776
became the model for all such bills as they
subsequently appeared in the Constitutions
of our States and Nation. Its distinguished author was
George Mason of Fairfax County, one of the leading
lawyers of his generation. Mason was under no illusions
about the place of God's law in the foundation of proper
human government. Four years before the Declaration
of Independence we find him arguing to the General
Court of Virginia that:

> "All acts of legislature apparently contrary to natural
> right and justice are, in our laws, and must be in the
> nature of things, considered as void. *The laws of
> nature are the laws of God, whose authority can be
> superseded by no power on earth.* A legislature must

* See Appendix Pages 116-121.

not obstruct our obedience to Him from whose punishments they cannot protect us. All human constitutions which contradict His (God's) laws, we are in
conscience bound to disobey."*

Like his associates in the distinguished fellowship we
now know as "The Founding Fathers" Mason understood
the futility of considering constitutions as ends in themselves. To command respect, obedience and continuity
"human constitutions" must implement and carry out
those

> "laws of God" which all *are in conscience bound*
> to obey.

**CUMULATIVE
EVIDENCE** At every step through the American
wilderness from Columbus to Kaskaskia,
from the first charter of Virginia to the
Declaration of Independence, the extremely practical
men who explored, settled and then united the States of
America made the promulgation and propagation of faith
and morals their chief and official reliance. William Penn,
the founder of Pennsylvania, epitomized the practical
faith and wisdom that went into the establishment of
America when he said that:

> "Those people who are not governed by God will be
> ruled by tyrants."

Penn knew that the only real and enduring protection
for liberty is in the firm religious faith of the people who
enjoy liberty. If we could stand with William Penn in the

*(1772, Robin v. Hardaway, 1 Jefferson 109.)

wilderness of 1683, and look at the long stream of human history in both directions—back to Herod and forward to Hitler—we would find that Penn was right. The record demonstrates that when God goes out of the people's government, a great vacuum is created which immediately sucks in a tyrant to take God's place.

DECISION OF THE SUPREME COURT There was no deviation from this conviction. More than 200 years after William Penn, the Supreme Court of the United States deciding the case of the Church of the Holy Trinity vs. the United States* asserted that:

> "This (the United States) is a religious people. This is historically true. From the discovery of America to this hour there is a single voice making this affirmation."

The decision then thoroughly reviews the fundamental documentary history of our country: the Charters, the Commissions, the official Proclamations, and finally the Constitutions of all the States of the Union. The Court then concludes:

> "There is no dissonance in these declarations. These are not individual sayings or declarations of private persons; they are organic utterances; they speak the voice of the entire people . . . There is a universal language pervading them all having but one meaning: they affirm and reaffirm *that this is a religious nation.*"

---

* (1892, 143 U. S. 457) See Appendix Pages 109-115.

DECLARATION REQUIRED There are doubtless many well adjusted "law abiding" people in America who are honestly skeptical about the validity of all Spiritual things including the existence of a personal God who rewards the good and punishes the wicked. It would shock these persons to their completely civilized fingertips if they were blandly asked to explain why they do not rob cash drawers, commit adultery and help themselves generally at the expense of their fellow men. The more astute among them will be able to rationalize their blameless conduct, but the truth is that their good life is

a *dividend from the trust fund of religious tradition*

built up for them by their God-fearing forebears. If these people have any doubt about the sentiments of their Revolutionary Forefathers, let them look at this provision from the first constitution of Pennsylvania (1776):

> "Each member of the assembly (legislature) before he takes his seat, shall make and subscribe the following declaration: 'I do believe in one God, the creator and governor of the Universe, the rewarder of the good and the punisher of the wicked'."

Similar provisions are found in the first constitutions of all the original States. The founders and builders of the great political fortune known as "Americanism" took no chances. From those who were to make American laws they demanded an irreducible minimum of faith.

CHAPTER FOUR

Democracy and the Republican Form

THE TRULY significant word symbols of Political Science, like rare pieces of priceless porcelain, should be used only when their use is appropriate. Even on these proper and rare occasions such terms should be handled with great care and consideration. The most meaningful word can be flattened out of all depth of precision by the ceaseless pounding of indiscriminate repetition.

Once upon a time the word "democracy" may have meant the same thing to all who spoke and heard it. Today, however, it is such a limp and vapid expression that the Russian Foreign Minister and the chairman of the Republican National Committee can both praise it highly on the self-same afternoon.

Any word that can be used at one and the same time to suggest the despotic political ideals of Soviet Russia and the treasured principles of Americanism has certainly lost every vestige of usefulness.

48

The word "democracy" has now become very much like the key to a highly exclusive private club which some waggish member caused to be secretly duplicated and widely distributed. Before the bona-fide "brothers" knew what was up, the plush and cosy clubhouse was swarming with all the questionable characters in the neighborhood. A disillusioned board of managers was finally forced to change the lock.

MEANINGLESS TERM Whatever significance may have been attached to it in the ancient past, the term "democracy" is not now a dependable key to the secret of a free society. Its continued use simply serves to make existing "confusion worse confounded" by giving notoriously tyrannical despotisms a distorted false face which seems to resemble American freedom. The friends and agents of these undeserving pretenders have given every encouragement to the currency of this word which dilutes the priceless and unique quality of Americanism by mixing and confusing it with the crude and forceful "leveling" devices of European politics.

The honest and serious students of American history will recall that our Founding Fathers managed to write both the Declaration of Independence and the Constitution of the United States without using the term "democracy" even once. No part of any one of the existing forty-eight State constitutions contains any reference to the word. Such men as John Adams, Madison, Hamilton, Jefferson and others who were most influential in the institution and formation of our government refer to "democracy" only to distinguish it sharply from the republican form of our American Constitutional System.

EXCLUSIVE FORM The Founding Fathers were not forgetting that the single official purpose of all American government is to secure and protect the unalienable God-given attributes of the individual human being, majorities to the contrary notwithstanding. Like Madison, Thomas Jefferson was convinced that this object and purpose of American government could best be accomplished through the republican form and he never ceased to praise the republicanism of the new Federal Constitution. On October 31, 1823, less than two years before his death, he wrote to a friend in Greece who had just sent him a new edition of Aristotle:

> "The equal rights of men and the happiness of every individual are now acknowledged to be the only legitimate objects of government. Modern times have the single advantage too, of having discovered the only device by which these rights can be secured, to wit: government by the people acting not in person but by representatives chosen by themselves."

To underscore the exclusively republican character of all American government the Federal Constitution itself says:

> "The United States shall guarantee to every State in the Union, a Republican Form of Government, and shall protect each of them against invasion."*

---

*(Art. IV, Sec. 4.)

Shakespeare has Juliet say truthfully that "a rose by any other name would smell as sweet." Many will therefore ask why the use of such a popular term as "democracy" may not be employed to serve the desirable convenience of putting all ramifications of our Free American society into a single word?

The answer is that the political system of our country is definitely in a class by itself.

No descriptive word which suggests or includes any existing political system in addition to our own will adequately describe the political system of the United States. On the contrary, the great majority of such words are fatally misleading, and in this respect the word "democracy" is one of the worst offenders.

DETERMINING DISTINCTION In both "form" and "substance" our American system is basically different from any politically organized society now or heretofore existing in the world. Thomas Jefferson attests this fact in the foregoing letter when he says that

"Modern times have the single advantage too, of having discovered the only device by which these rights can be secured."

The "rights," namely the unalienable rights of each person in the land, constitute the "substance" of American government. The "device" by which these rights can be secured is the American "form" of government. The conjunction of this "form" and this "substance" was unique and new in Jefferson's time and it is completely unique today.

A Republican form of government strictly and constitutionally dedicated to the protection of the God-given unalienable rights of men appeared in the world for the first time with the organization of the United States of America. This "form" was then and there composed and designed to hold and contain its precious substance.

> The indissoluble union of this form and this substance equals Americanism and it equals nothing else.

No useful and informative purpose is served by tossing this singular and exclusive American development into all or any of such meaningless generalizations as "freedom-loving-democratic- Anti-Fascist Peoples of the World." This is not to say that we are selfishly and officially allergic to the ideal of the world wide human brotherhood.

> On the contrary Americanism offers the only valid formula for the ultimate achievement of that ideal.

The basis of this formula is the indestructible God-given human personality which is the one thing that every American definitely and officially holds in common with each human being on Earth. It is unfortunate that this is also the one thing that every political system in the Un-American world officially and categorically denies.

BY THEIR FRUITS By their perennial harvest of bitter fruits these foreign governmental systems are shown to be fatally wrong. Since the time that America was discovered the *power* of these systems has shifted from autocratic kings to political or parliamentary ministers. At the moment all the governing politicians, premiers, ministers and magistrates of Europe pretend to be devoted to "popular" government and some of them hold office as the result of popular elections. Nevertheless, from the autocratic kings to the conscienceless commissars, European political science has always held consistently to the proposition that government, once installed,

is unlimited in its power over its subjects.

The continuing and controlling principle of European politics has thus been BIG AND ALL POWERFUL GOVERNMENT which does not recognize and consequently need not respect any such thing as an *unalienable right in the individual citizen.*

More than one hundred years before the French Revolution, the then ruling royal autocrat of France, Louis XIV declared "*I* am the State." His BIG AND ALL POWERFUL GOVERNMENT was thus entirely personal and the individual Frenchman could expect only such "liberty" as King Louis chose to extend to him. Two hundred years later, the European Karl Marx, prophet of the modern Socialist-Communist political and economic dispensation, disposed of the individual citizen in these words:

> "The democratic concept of man is false, because it is Christian. The democratic concept holds that each man is a sovereign being. This is the *illusion, dream* and *postulate* of Christianity."

One hundred years after Karl Marx thus wrote off the importance of the individual human personality in that derisive condemnation of Christianity, Adolf Hitler made his decisive bid for the control of Europe on what he represented to be a drive *against Communism*. Nevertheless this is what Hitler said about the unalienable rights of the individual man:

> "To the Christian doctrine of infinite significance of the individual human soul, I oppose with icy clarity the saving doctrine of the *nothingness and insignificance of the human being*."

LOUIS, MARX AND HITLER Students of political science would probably be hard pressed to find a recognized modern "authority" who puts Louis XIV, Karl Marx and Adolf Hitler into the same political bed. Nevertheless, on the *vital* principle of BIG AND ALL POWERFUL GOVERNMENT with no inherent responsibility for or duty toward the individual human being, these important European characters were in perfect accord.

The disappearance of Hitler has brought no observable change in European political ideals. Since the end

of the war, England has moved *officially* into the orbit
of the all-powerful States, while on the European Continent, both East and West of the "Iron Curtain," the
"nothingness and insignificance of the human being" is
everything that Adolph Hitler could have wished for.

If BIG AND ALL POWERFUL GOVERNMENT was the
secret of general popular welfare, Europe would have
always been the land of milk and honey, while the history
of the United States would be a story of general misery,
poverty and destitution. The facts are the other way
round. Europe's record proves that BIG AND ALL POWER-
FUL GOVERNMENT, whether its sanction be royal, "democratic" or revolutionary, produces general warfare instead
of general welfare and promotes penury and pestilence
rather than progress and prosperity.

**COMPROMISE
SUICIDAL**
The all-time record discloses that where-
soever government gets bigger and bigger and more and more powerful it moves
at the same time and at the same speed toward the hellish
goal of Adolf Hitler, namely, the "nothingness and insignificance" of the individual human being. Modern
English history shows that "democracy" is no inherent
and absolute defense against the pernicious increase of
governmental strength.

It is not *how* the government gets its power but the
amount of power it gets that determines the fate of each
and every individual John Doe who lives under its juris-

diction. The God-given nature of the said John Doe lays upon all human government a drastic and vital set of limitations. In the United States these limitations are written into Constitutions which all of our governments must observe. In Europe no such limitations are acknowledged. This is the precise issue between the foreign systems of power politics and the American system of personalized justice. The issue is both sharp and pointed. Efforts to blunt or compromise it by the use of "democracy" to describe both systems are worse than useless. Such attempts discredit Americanism by making its distinctive architecture look like the standard model for European Power Houses.

IRREPARABLE LOSS We do not serve the cause of international peace and world wide understanding by deliberately obscuring the essential fundamental cleavage between Americanism and Europeanism. On the contrary, when we shade or soften the sharp line which separates our system from theirs, we risk a great loss at home and with no possibility of compensating gain to any of our foreign neighbors. Real and permanent world order must be built upon a system which insures the universal dispensation of personal man to man justice. This means that individual rights, the substance of our system, must be acknowledged and protected by the government of every state in the world. Outside of the United States there is no source from which un-American peoples can learn about such a system. If they are led to believe that there is no essential difference between their governments and ours their political aspirations will continue to center upon

> "The good old rule, the simple plan, that they should take who have the power and they should keep who can."

There is every reason to believe that Republican forms of government, every branch of which is constitutionally committed to the protection of unalienable individual rights, could and would permanently solve the political aches and pains of the whole world. But there, as here and everywhere, mere form without substance must collapse of its own weight. The obvious and peculiar blessings of American life which so many thoughtlessly attribute to our American "form" of government, would automatically disappear if the "purpose" and "object" of that form were suddenly changed or withdrawn. Regardless of the beauty of its shape and design an empty glass offers no consolation to a desperately thirsty man. In like manner the American form of government when emptied of its substantial element of personal rights and personal justice is stripped of every logical excuse for its continued existence.

INTENTIONAL INEFFICIENCY Considered merely as a governmental mechanism, separate and apart from its special purpose, singular object and essential substance, the American form of government is the most cumbersome and inefficient system ever put into operation. Its separate and distinct authorities are divided into six mutually exclusive water-tight compartments, namely the legislature, executive and judiciary of both the State and Federal Governments. Regardless of the urgency of public business no one of these authorities may encroach upon the other. From the sum total of these divided powers are subtracted important specifications of two separate bills of personal rights, one prefixed to the Constitution of the State, the other appended to the Constitution of the Federal Government.

The salient feature of this famed form of government is an involved system of so-called "checks and balances." Congress checks the President and vice versa while the Federal Courts check both. On the State side, the legislature checks the governor who in turn checks the legislature while both are checked by the State Courts. In addition to these checks, the whole power of the Federal Government is restrained by the reserved powers of the States. These powers in turn are perpetually balanced against those granted to the Federal Government in the Federal Constitution.

Seen in perspective, this constitutional system, which is our American form of government, is a veritable latticework of barbed wire entanglements thrown around every governmental official in the land. It is a pattern of slow motion and inefficiency which no "expediter" would tolerate for five minutes in any private business organization. Is it any wonder therefore that the eager-beavers of modern jurisprudence chafe under these impediments to prompt and efficient public service? What possible answer can be made to the ever swelling chorus which demands that our *antiquated* form of government be *streamlined* toward centralized authority and sharpened responsibility? There is no answer—except one. That answer is drawn from the *substance* which this complicated *form* was built to hold safe and secure.

PURPOSE CLEAR   The men who fashioned this form of government were thinking of John Doe's life, liberty and pursuit of happiness. Their principal concern was not with the efficiency of government, but with the safety of the God-created human personality. These Founding Fathers knew that the most *efficient* government on earth is that of an absolute and unrestricted despotism. They had learned their political science the hard way. In their own experience they had discovered that the God-given liberty of the individual citizen inevitably withers and disappears under the tender ministrations of an unrestricted government. Between the disorders of anarchy and the inevitable despotic development of the best-intentioned un-limited government they chose the golden mean. The resulting American form is a series of *servant-governments* all charged with the duty of protecting personal rights and enforcing personal duties.

The Founding Fathers loaded these new servant-governments with limitations and restrictions calculated to keep all of their noses to the grindstone of their fundamental purpose and prevent them from using their necessary tools to destroy what the servants were hired to preserve. The Framers made sure that the rights of one man could be maintained against other men but they also made sure that those same rights could be asserted at all times *against the power of government* itself. They knew that it is in the very nature of every government to resent this last assertion as an affront to its sovereign dignity. Hence, they tied the new servant-governments down into their proper place by a system of strong checks and balances. In addition to extended bills of personal rights they limited one government by another government and each of their branches by another branch. They thus protected the citizen by rivalries and divisions within the governmental structure itself.

THE TEST OF THE PUDDING Within its designated sphere of constitutionally allotted powers and subject always to its guiding purpose as stated in the Declaration of Independence, American government was designed to function through representatives chosen either directly or indirectly by the people, and responsible to the people on regularly recurring election days. This *representative system* is the essence of the *Republican Form* of government to which all of the Founding Fathers were so enthusiastically devoted. In State and Federal constitutions they deliberately withheld from the people the right to directly and "democratically" decide governmental questions for themselves. The Founders would have been appalled at the idea of *rubber stamp* legislators, *office boy* executives or *pressure* *group* government on the Federal or State level. Thomas Jefferson, whose political ideas were considerably more "democratic" than any of his contemporaries, wrote in 1816

> "that (the people) being unqualified for the man-
> agement of affairs requiring intelligence above the
> common level, yet competent judges of human char-
> acter, (they) chose for their management representa-
> tives, some by themselves immediately, others by
> electors chosen by themselves. Action by citizens in
> person, in affairs within their reach and competence,
> and in all others by representatives chosen imme-
> diately and removable by themselves (the people)
> constitutes the essence of a Republic."

EFFICIENCY vs. FREEDOM Those who do not share the Founding Fathers' devotion to the unalienable sacredness of the human personality, will regard this form of government as a crazy quilt of cross purposes. Such persons will argue quite plausibly for a new type of government immediately re-sponsible to "the people" in which the administrative and legislative functions are blended for efficiency while the courts are relegated to the simple duty of resolving quarrels between private individuals. These advocates of the "democratic process" maintain that in such a stream-lined system society would have the only protection to which it is logically entitled, namely, frequent and free elections. This is the system that prevailed in England at the time of the American Revolution, and it is exactly the kind of government that Socialist England has today. The American form and the English form have thus worked side by side in the same world for more than 150 years. From the separate inventories of their respective accomplishments, you may take your ultimate choice. Meanwhile, Americans are asked to devise new and more generous "Marshall Plans" for the further American relief of England and other so-called "democratic" nations throughout the world.

Private Enterprise

Excepting only admitted Communists and extreme Socialists no American who debates the merits of Private Enterprise ever opposes it squarely and entirely.

It is obvious, of course, that the complete destruction of Private Enterprise would call for the substitution of its alternative, namely Public Enterprise in all branches of commerce and industry. Everyone seems to agree that such complete public ownership of all business would be "un-American." That unpopular position is consequently left open for professional revolutionaries. Thus, between "laissez-faire," which no one defends, and complete public ownership of industry, which no one advocates, there are a hundred thousand little fortresses of individual opinion each one a bit more "American" and/or "democratic" than another. However, it is entirely possible to answer correctly this question of Private Enterprise by the selfless logic of basic Americanism.

THE KEY TO PEACE

AVAILABILITY OF RESOURCES The basic controlling principle of Americanism is the unalienable God-given personality of the individual human being. If the beliefs of our forefathers were valid

> this world and everything in it was designed and made to help this creature keep an Eternal rendezvous with his Creator by a judicious exercise of his unalienable personal liberty.

If he were alone in the Universe this man's personal dominion over all these things would be complete and unquestioned. But it was "not good for man to be alone." For the better fulfillment of his immortal destiny he was increased and multiplied into a "society" of men. Since this increase and multiplication was an execution of God's design it is inconceivable that He would have enclosed these indestructible personalities within a realm of resources insufficient for the rational life of each and all of them. There must be enough of these resources to go around and for the same reason the Creator must intend that they should go around.

At all times therefore, each man must have personal access to the necessities of life. A human institution or system which fences any man off from what is required to sustain him would unlawfully deprive that man of what our Declaration of Independence calls an "unalienable right."

RIGHTS AND RESPONSIBILITIES Americanism acknowledges that each man has a God-given right and duty to live out his allotted span of years. If any one is able but unwilling to sustain his life that is his own funeral, literally as well as figuratively. However, if such a man is *anxious* but *unable* to sustain himself, then in that event, his neighbor has a natural God-imposed obligation to help him. Since human life is an unalienable attribute we can neither take it from ourself by suicide nor from our neighbor by murdering him. When we permit our neighbor to starve for want of food he cannot obtain while we are in a position to supply it, we kill him just as effectively as if we had hit him with a club. Americanism consequently demands that when our neighbor is destitute we must assist him.

If you have had the ability, industry, and good fortune to accumulate a surplus of goods, the possible future destitution of your neighbor thus operates as a perpetual lien upon those surplus accumulations. Your right to that surplus is not absolute because if it was absolute you could conscientiously hold it all for yourself alone and let your neighbor starve. In the latter situation you would, in effect, alienate your neighbor's life, whereas the Declaration of Independence says that his life is unalienable.

PRIVATE PROP-ERTY ESSENTIAL Since you are thus naturally and morally obliged to help your neighbor in his unfortunate destitution may you shirk this social responsibility by deliberately keeping yourself so poor that you are never in a position to help anybody but yourself? By wilfully avoiding the accumulation of an economic surplus you are flouting your neighbor's rights, in two ways. In the first place you are wilfully risking the possibility that your own sudden destitution may throw a burden upon him. In the second place, your deliberate and wilful improvidence will make it impossible for you to assist him in the unfortunate event of his destitution. It follows therefore that each responsible human being has both a natural right and a natural duty to acquire and hold private property. Any other hypothesis would disregard the sacred unalienable character of human life.

This natural right of the individual person to acquire and hold property must be respected and upheld by everybody. We have seen that American government is merely an agency for the protection of human rights, consequently it is the duty of American government to protect this natural right in every person within its jurisdiction. Like all other personal rights this one must be exercised consistently with the equal rights of others. We must consequently make our first personal acquisitions of property either from some natural unappropriated stock or from the stock of some other person with the latter's full agreement and consent.

PROPERTY LIMITLESS When the human population of the world was thin and widely scattered, the property acquisitions of individual persons were made chiefly from the vast unclaimed resources of nature. In our own time practically all of these resources have been taken into private ownership. Nevertheless the human population of the world continues to increase. Millions of propertyless persons become of age every year. As we have seen, each of these persons holds a natural right of access to the necessities of life as well as a natural right and duty to acquire and hold a store of private property for himself. Shall we therefore divide the existing store of privately held property among all the people of the Earth? This expedient would unquestionably violate the natural rights of present holders, and instead of solving the problem posed by the ever increasing number of propertyless people it would complicate that problem beyond any possibility of solution. Such division would necessarily be a continuous process which would paralyze the productivity of the world's resources in one generation.

It is not by dividing and diminishing the shares of what we have, but rather by multiplying them intensively that the total wealth of the world is increased at the same time that new private shares are made possible for each individual person.

For instance, it is relatively well established that the area of the Earth's surface has not been increased since the time of its creation. It is likewise highly probable that the total amount of its purely natural resources has continued to diminish since man first came upon the Earth. But it is definitely and unquestionably certain that since Adam's time the unnatural man-made resources of this world have been increased far beyond our powers of estimation. By the design of his Creator, man multiplied not merely his own species but every species of property as well. It is obvious that this process of property production must be continuously accelerated otherwise the supply of necessary goods would soon be exhausted by the increase in human population.

REPRODUCTION AND PROPERTY We know that an all-wise Providence has safely insured the reproduction of human beings by the universal implantation of sex impulses. Since physical goods must increase proportionately with human life it is equally natural and universal that impetus for the increased production of property is provided. This impetus is evidenced in the eagerness of each man and all men to own and control material things. This natural and necessary "eagerness" in each individual is sometimes referred to as "The Profit Motive." It might be more properly called the *incentive impulse*.

As he grows into the full stature of responsibility each person is thus eager to expend his energy for those goods that are necessary and desirable to fulfill his unalienable responsibilities. With the consent of its owners he operates upon the existing store of capital property with useful productive work. The result is that "two blades of grass grow where one grew before." New stores of Private Property are thus created and diffused through each new generation. Without this productive multiplication of the world's resources the human race would long since have died of sheer starvation. There is no time in human history when a mere division of all available property would have served to keep the population alive for one short generation. A ceaseless Process of production and reproduction is thus responsible for the continuity of unalienable human life upon Earth.

THE ESSENTIAL INGREDIENTS There are three natural and necessary ingredients for the required volume of this indispensable productive process. The first of these is a constantly growing capital stock of tools and raw materials. The second is ample and readily available supplies of human labor, human ingenuity, and human genius. The third is the insatiable *incentive impulse* in each human being to own and control property. Without ingredient number three, no adequate stock of number one would ever exist and number two would degenerate into Edwin Markham's graphic and gloomy poem picture "The Man With the Hoe"—except that the hoe would be missing.

Like the vital and necessary *sex impulse* this invaluable and necessary *incentive impulse* must be exercised within the limits of the natural law from which it proceeds. Both impulses are subject to restraints in the interests of justice and morality, but it would be foolish and futile to deny the existence and necessity of either or both of them.

Sex reproduction in the normal and natural family life of human beings has been and is the cornerstone of practically all civilization. Each person knows that he personally has something very vital to lose through the establishment of unnatural controls upon the sex impulse and so he is against such proposals. But many of the same people will applaud proposals which do violence to the "incentive impulse" by making the state the absolute manager, if not the owner, of all private property enterprises. These same people are impressed by socialistic proposals to confiscate all business profits forgetting that reasonable profits are the necessary and proper result of the natural incentive impulse in the same way that children are the result of the sex impulse of human beings. The difference in this popular reaction to the sex impulse on the one hand and the incentive impulse on the other is explained by the incentive impulse itself. The incentive impulse is the desire to gain something for one's self and many people feel that they have "something to gain" by the establishment of governmental restrictions on incentive. If they perceived that the principle of both suggestions is the same, namely the power of state to invade necessary natural rights and duties, they would be just as opposed to one proposition as they are to the other.

POPULATION AND SUPPLIES As long as the natural sex impulse operates to produce the population of the world the natural incentive impulse must operate just as freely to produce sufficient goods to feed, clothe and shelter that population. Any proposal to bring unreasonable restrictions upon *either* of these impulses is a proposal to violate natural rights. A state that can logically and validly establish the one can just as logically and validly establish the other. The government is either the servant of human nature as the Declaration of Independence says it is, or it is the absolute boss and manager of human nature as the Communists say it is.

The stultification of the incentive impulse will and must react violently against the productive processes of any society that adopts it. On the contrary, the productive multiplication of physical goods increases in direct proportion to the freedom of private individual enterprise. It is no mere coincidence that the industrial revolution with its great upsurge in productive processes appeared promptly in the wake of the American Declaration of Independence.

PRIVATE ENTERPRISE AND BOUNTY   It is to the private enterprise of American men and women that an enslaved and starving world looks today for food and sustenance. If state-owned and state-controlled economies could out-produce private enterprise uncounted millions of men and women would not have died of starvation in Soviet Russia since 1920. Neither would we now be considering the indefinite extension of the "Marshall Plan" every dollar of all of which is in addition to the more than Fifty Billion Dollars worth of goods that we have donated to foreign governments since the end of World War II.

In spite of all this we find that in the confused jargon of our private enterprise debate a man is called "progressive" the minute he starts shooting at the only remaining goose that lays golden eggs. In the same discussion the "common man" is recruited en masse against the one system which has consistently offered men a chance to become "uncommon."

Proposed alternatives to private enterprise all add up to a super-state which will sterilize the natural incentive impulse of human beings with a system of complete government endowed "security."

Just as the nub of private enterprise is freedom, so is slavery the inevitable alternative.

For an unidentified benefit deceptively termed "freedom from fear" we are asked to surrender freedom itself.

Americanism and Communism

O UR MOST respected "experts" are now protesting against our reiteration of the obvious fact that the United States is the freest, richest and most powerful country on earth. They declare that such statements merely serve to spread narrow and selfish nationalism at a time when we should think only in terms of a peaceful and unified world community. This warning is additional evidence of the widely prevailing misunderstanding about the source and nature of our American social order.

The critics say that the freedom, riches and power of the United States are ill-gotten gains from the ruthless exploitation of lavish natural resources and that we should be ashamed of them. The truth is that a great many other countries, including Russia, are much richer in natural resources than the United States has ever been. In proportion to our population, we have slightly less than our fair share of such natural resources as land, forests and water power. We have a great deal less than our share of such things as natural rubber, tin, nickel and a long list of vital basic minerals. Natural resources have had little if anything to do with the accumulation of wealth, freedom and power in the United States. These great advantages are simply the end result of *basic American principles* as applied through our enlightened and distinctively different constitutional system.

JUSTIFIABLE PRIDE We praise these rich fruits precisely to call attention to the tree upon which they were produced and to advertise the high quality of the soil in which the tree was planted. We cite these results in recommendation of the means through which the results were obtained. Thus, an outspoken and understanding pride in American achievements is the first and best contribution that we can make to the establishment of comparable conditions throughout the world.

Let us ask the apprehensive experts a few questions. If and when a specific cure for cancer is discovered in the United States, will its announcement be another manifestation of "narrow nationalism"? Should we conceal the facts about this great American accomplishment out of consideration for other countries not yet in on the secret? Or, on the contrary, should we widely publicize all authenticated cures as fast as they occur? These questions answer themselves. By advertising the success of our treatment we would excite world interest in its theory and method. Foreign scientists would soon be employing the new American technique. In this manner our discovery would benefit not only ourselves, but all the people in the world. Unfortunately, we do not now have such a cure for cancer but we do have a specific and demonstrated cure for many of the most deadly and persistent ills of Human Society. Our sick and disordered neighbors in the "world community" will never believe this to the point of taking the "cure" until they are confronted with unmistakable evidence of our robust and persistent health as sharply contrasted with their chronic illnesses.

ABUNDANCE AND FAMINE Repeated comparison of American abundance with foreign famine consequently serves many necessary and practical purposes. First of all, for the benefit of our citizens, it underscores the astounding but indisputable fact that the poorest person in the United States has immeasurably more of the basic necessities and comforts of life than ninety-five per cent of all of the people who live in the rest of the world. Of the more than two billion persons residing outside of the United States, only the Molotovs, the Titos, the Nabobs, the small number of the ever more and more precarious Plutocrats and a mere handful of others fare better than people on the lowest level of our American standard of living. If Americans themselves give little or no consideration to this striking phenomenon, how can we expect the sick and disillusioned foreigners to know about it?

It would be heartless bad taste, certainly, for healthy, well-fed people to flex their mighty muscles before the hopelessly ill and undernourished. On the contrary, it is logical and commendable for a healthy person to cite his own vigor and vitality as a recommendation for the thing that keeps him in that condition. This is particularly true when the thing recommended is the only thing that will improve the person to whom it is offered.

There is but one justifiable hope for a world community of free and reasonably prosperous people. That hope lies in the ultimate acceptance of American principles by all the peoples of the earth. The whole world must be convinced, first, that we are the strongest, richest and freest nation of all history; second, that this happy, unprecedented condition is the necessary consequence of the fixed true principle upon which our society was founded and by which it is governed.

COMMON DENOMINATOR Those who understand it know that this American principle is neither local, narrow nor merely national. On the contrary, it is naturally diffusive and as broad as human nature itself. American Principle is the one demonstrated common denominator of all mankind. It declares that "all men"—not just Americans—"are *created* equal." It does not spend itself in a pious hope for the ultimate community of nations but rather proclaims and establishes a presently existing brotherhood of all men under the common Fatherhood of God. Its ideal is not embodied in a vague and meaningless "democracy" but in a true *self-government* of each individual, by himself through his conscience, under God.

This is what James Madison, The Father of the Constitution, meant when he said that

> "we rest all our political experiments on the *capacity of mankind for self-government.*"

To American principle the State is a servile and secondary thing which picks up where conscience unfortunately falls down. George Washington led the applause of the Founding Fathers when on the eve of the Declaration of Independence Thomas Paine wrote that

> "government like dress is the badge of lost innocence; the palaces of Kings are built upon the ruins of the bowers of paradise."

Paine thus charged up government to the blight of original sin and gave to virtue and good conscience the complete credit for freedom and self-government. American principle absorbed this concept completely. It underscored Paine's conclusion that

> "were the impulses of conscience clear and irresistibly obeyed man would need no other law-giver."

GOVERNMENT A NECESSARY EVIL While Europeanism was worshipping the State as the masterful source of justice, order, property and rights of all kinds, Americanism from its inception accepted political government as a necessary evil. Madison called government "the greatest of all reflections on human nature." Thus as Americans advance in the civilizing arts and restraints of self-government through progressively strengthened consciences, Americanism envisions a proportionate shrinkage of the State as an important factor in the American Social Order. This is the genesis of the American truism that those people are governed best who are governed least. In its converse this statement is likewise true, for certainly those people are best who require the least government.

In a community of saints the Moral Law would be the only law needed to provide such a community with perfect peace, complete order and universal justice. It is only when such a community is invaded by amoral or immoral people—or when some of the saints fall from grace—that man made regulations are required to hold the immoral or amoral elements in line.

EXAMPLES OF DEMORALIZATION   How any segment of society functions when it has been officially demoralized was demonstrated in Germany under the Nazis just as it is now being demonstrated in Russia under the Communists. In spite of the officially unmoral character of both Nazism and Communism, the people who lived in Hitler's Germany like those who now live in Communist Russia, were and are human beings with a full inheritance of human and moral inclinations. It has been impossible for the Russian Dictatorship—just as it was impossible for Hitler—to remove from people in one generation what has been ingrained in the race for hundreds of years, namely, a moral conscience.

STALIN'S BODYGUARD   We are told authoritatively that the overwhelming majority of the Russian people still believe in God and that considerably less than five per cent of the entire population are tested and accepted members of the Communist (and therefore atheist) *elect*. Hitler had to cull his clique of conspirators very carefully to find characters sufficiently demoralized to take charge of Buchenwald and Dachau. Today, and in spite of its official atheism, the Russian Communist dictatorship profits immeasurably from the inherited predisposition to moral restraints. These prevent millions of the harried and harassed victims of that dictatorship from falling upon their captors and killing them in cold blood. Russia's omnipresent army of secret police needs to watch only those who would *otherwise* resort to violent and murderous protest. Thus, ironically, Religion continues to be Stalin's best and most effective bodyguard.

PROFESSED OBJECTIVES   It is ironical, to say the least, that the trend of Americanism toward the eventual stateless society, is likewise the professed ultimate end of Americanism's most deadly and challenging enemy, Communism. Marxist Communism predicts that the State will eventually "wither away" and disappear. Political government will end, it says, when the state, personified in the dictatorship of the proletariat, has completed the job of ruthlessly liquidating all other classes of society. Once this liquidation is completed, only pure proletarians will remain. Since, under communism, the State's sole purpose is to protect the proletarian "class" by exterminating other "predatory capitalistic classes" the state will automatically die when its task of extermination is completed.

Nothing more clearly illustrates the diametric opposition of Communism to Americanism than this apparent similarity of their ultimate ends.

> Communism would establish a peaceful classless society of proletarians by killing off all enemy classes. Americanism *dissolves* class conflicts by *indoctrinating each man* and thereby diffusing through *all men* the true concept of human brotherhood.

Communism sees human life as a battlefield of irreconcilable "group" interests. Americanism proclaims that human life is a common ground upon which the moral claims and duties of each man are to be reconciled with the reciprocal claims and duties of every other man. Communism is a philosophy of Hate. Americanism is a basic lesson in love. One is a blueprint for peace through violence; the other is a formula for individual freedom in the exercise of peaceful and mutual self-restraint.

The impact of Communism against Americanism is the old collision of individual rights with the demands of Society. Communism merely amplifies the noise of this collision through the modern loud-speakers of dialectical materialism. Communism disposes of the individual personality at the very outset by herding it into high-walled, escape-proof compartments called "classes." These "classes" are then deliberately incited one against the other in the technique of an old-fashioned battle-royal. Next comes the orgy of mass murder, which the Communists call "liquidation of the predatory classes" to be followed by the unchallenged domination of the "proletariat."

FATAL ERROR Americanism senses that the great error of Communism is not committed at the murderous end of its brutal and bloody road but at its very beginning. In its organization and purpose Communism makes the only fundamental mistake that it is possible for any political and social system to commit. It comes up at the outset with the wrong answers to the controlling questions presented to every political system by the very *nature* of the human beings with whom it proposes to deal:

1—Does the system exist for the individual man or does the individual man exist for the system?

2—Is the social order more important than the people it embraces, or is it the other way around?

3—Does John Doe have personal individual rights which the system is bound to respect and if so, can he force the system to protect them, or is John Doe an indistinguishable part of a "mass," "class" or "group" of the total Society?

Communism, along with Fascism, Nazism, Socialism and every form of Statism, answers:

1—Man exists for the system.

2—The social order is all important.

3—The individual John Doe has no rights that the system is bound to respect.

Thus, in Communism, as in despotism generally, the individual as a person is completely lost in the government. His very life's blood is transfused into the governing body for the exclusive use and purpose of that body. Communism frankly admits that it is a completely materialistic conception. It insists that man is merely matter; oil in the engine or cogs on the wheels. The entity is the machine and the machine is the dictatorship.

INTELLECTUALS AND THE WEALTHY We pay Communism an undeserved compliment when we think and speak of it as "The Poor Man's Club" and concede that it is a simple and normal reaction against economic oppression and injustice. The facts would seem to go the other way. In this period which has been called one of "unprecedented general prosperity" we are more seriously threatened by Communism and Communists than we have ever been at any time in our history. There is more Communism and there are more Communists in America today than we had in the deepest trough of the Great Depression in the Nineteen Thirties.

Many of our most rabid and influential American Communists are in the very highest income tax brackets year after year. When Communism's top flight undercover agents are exposed they are not discovered in the so-called "underprivileged groups" of the country. On the contrary in practically every instance they are found to be persons of superior education with excellent social, financial and political connections. How is this to be explained? St.

Augustine explained it fifteen hundred years ago when he said:

> "The desire to rule over our equals is an intolerable lust of the soul."

Communism is just another manifestation of this age-old Devil-made lust for power. It is an activation of the hellish principle of tyranny just as Americanism is the activation of the Godly principle of personal liberty.

THE ONLY ALTERNATIVE For this precise mechanistic theory of the social order there is but one effective and logical alternative. That alternative is the concept of each man as a divinely created spirit with a special mission on earth and an immortal destiny hereafter. In the practical political order this alternative is known as "Americanism" which regards this sacred human personality as the central control point of God's creative purpose. In the Philosophy of Americanism, each man was created for Eternity with everything on earth, and especially the government, set up and ordained to help him to that final end. In this philosophy and pursuant to this principle, groups, classes, races and nations of men are merely accidental; only the individual is fundamental and substantial.

LIMITLESS IN APPLICATION This American individualism is neither selfishly personal nor narrowly nationalistic. As a matter of fact, Americanism goes Internationalism one better. Americanism seeks not merely a community of *nations* but a world wide *community of men* whose God-given unalienable rights and whose intrinsically worthwhile human personalities are respected and protected by *all* of the institutions of this earth, but particularly by governments and states. Moreover, Americanism is ready with acceptable proofs to show that its grand ideal is no wild impractical hallucination. To the Communists who charge that this doctrine produces merely "Pie in the sky" Americanism answers that in its short, active life to date it has exalted the spirits of hundreds of millions of men who all the while were better housed, better fed, better clothed and better paid than men have ever been before in the long history of the world.

All the while, the magic of Americanism's political catalysis has blended the heretofore unmixable oil and water of other lands—the fighting races, the fighting classes, the fighting creeds, the clashing colors—into a clear solution of common citizenship. The German, the English, the Irish, the Italian, the Polish, the Aristocratic and Proletarian element in each prospective American has been officially stripped from him at the ocean's edge of the United States. Then and there, by application of the catalytic agency of American principle, race consciousness, class consciousness and group consciousness officially disappear. The result is the perfection of all creation—a man, equal before his God, and *for that reason* equal before the law of his land.

British Statism

SIR WILLIAM BLACKSTONE, the great interpreter of the English common law, states in his celebrated commentaries that:

> "When the supreme Being formed the universe, and created matter out of nothing, he impressed certain principles upon that matter, from which it can never depart, and without which it would cease to be."

Each thing on earth is impressed with principles that are inseparable from that thing. From and upon these principles definite unchangeable laws are projected and the thing in question must observe these laws of its nature in all of its movements and applications.

American principles are *right* because they are in harmony with the nature of human beings with whom these principles are concerned. The principles of Socialism, Communism and Fascism are wrong precisely because they deny these basic natural principles of mankind. Nothing can prevent the successful practical operation of American principles if we apply them intelligently in the reasoned conviction that *since they are right they must be preserved*. On the contrary, no amount of sacrifice, faith or fanaticism on the part of their adherents can make any form of "Statism" work successfully in practice for the reason that the successful operation of the basic false principle in all forms of Statism would contradict nature and thus frustrate the end and purpose for which human beings are created.

THE NATURE OF STATISM "Statism" is a comparatively new word for an institution that is as old as the human race. It appears on every page of recorded history but in disguises and with formal variations that are seldom if ever repeated. Like the constantly changing surface of the essentially changeless sea, Statism may be brutal or benevolent, cruel or compassionate, in turn or in combination. But regardless of its transient moods, Statism always and everywhere is the embodiment of tyrannical, capricious and unlimited government whose subjects are legally powerless to resist its decrees. In sheer desperation the subjects may and often do embrace one form of Statism as a means of protection or liberation from another form. Thus, Hitler was raised to absolute power in Germany by people who feared the menace of Communism.

CHANGING HORSES Approximately two hundred years before Hitler was born the people of England made the same sort of an exchange in their "glorious revolution" of 1688. It was in the course of this

revolution that the autocratic King James II was driven
from England. Then at the invitation of the British Parliament, King William and Queen Mary of Orange
crossed the channel and mounted the vacant British
throne. To the Englishmen of that day this all seemed
to be a liberation of the very highest order. Many years
passed before they fully realized that in making the mon-
archy completely subservient to Parliament, they surrendered the whole bundle of effective rights against government that they had developed and accumulated against
the King through the centuries beginning with Magna
Charta.

After 1688 the British crown was no longer a threat to
the liberties of Englishmen but in the "glorious revolution" Parliament came out on the top of the British
Governmental structure *with completely unlimited power*.
By this time each of the American Colonies had been
established by the personal charter of the King of England. These charters made each of the colonies self governing for all practical purposes and the intervening
ocean temporarily immunized them from direct attack by
Parliamentary legislation. Thus, the English revolution of
1688 had no practical effect in America except perhaps
to send a few adherents of James II scurrying here for
asylum.

Parliament was cautious and conservative in the use of
its newfound absolutism. After all, it was, in part, an elec-
tive body whose members had to live with their constitu-
ents. Englishmen gradually assimilated the significant

change that had taken place in their political system, but the American colonists did not learn its full implications until 1765 when Parliament passed the infamous Stamp Act. Then began the frantic protests; "Tea Parties" and petitions "to the King from his loyal American subjects." The over-all complaint was against the violation of their Royal charters by the "pretended legislation" of a "jurisdiction foreign to our Constitutions and unacknowledged by our laws."

COLONISTS ASSERT RIGHTS Against the usurpations of Parliament the Colonists asserted their "immemorial rights as Englishmen" as these rights had been adjudicated by Lord Chief Justice Coke in years prior to 1688. Parliament responded by announcing the established fact that no Englishman had any right that Parliament was bound to respect and to prove it Parliament repealed the Charter of Massachusetts (1774). Since they apparently had no rights as Englishmen, the Americans fell back upon their rights under "the laws of Nature and of Nature's God." They so declared their independence and fought the war of the revolution.

The government of England was not "Socialistic" in 1776, nor were its practices extremely "tyrannical" by the comparisons available at the time. Throughout the American Revolution there were many people in England and America who felt that a suitable compromise of the English-American differences could and should be worked out between the "Mother Country" and her colonies, but responsible American leadership saw with Thomas Paine, that the freedom of Englishmen depended solely upon "the virtue of Parliament." For these leaders the "virtue" of even the best government is no adequate protection for the free nature of men. To the Tories or "Loyalists" this was an excuselessly doctrinaire attitude completely divorced from the realities. These appeasers argued that the *practice* rather than the *principle* should control the judgment of such an important controversy. Nevertheless, and fortunately, the adherents of principle prevailed. Today, the "practices" of the British government constitute one more convincing proof that the adherents of principle were correct.

PRISONERS ON PAROLE The American Colonies refused to knuckle under to British Statism. Their British brethren did knuckle under. In the intervening years the omnipotent British parliament has moved from conservative imperialism to radical Socialism. Yet at no point along the line has any Englishman been able legally to challenge any action by his government regardless of the effect of such action upon that Englishman's person, liberty or property.

When and where such unlimited government prevails human freedom is banished and the citizens of such a government are merely prisoners on parole. It is then for the government alone to decide upon the conditions of the parole and for what period or periods it shall be extended. In this respect for many years the British Parliament was extremely generous—*with Englishmen*. In India, Ireland, Africa, Malaya and elsewhere throughout the far-flung British possessions "on which the sun never set" it was often a different story. In those areas the British subjects realized their plight as clearly as the Americans did in 1776, but unlike the Americans, they lacked the means, the will or both effectively to do something about it.

The all-powerful British Parliament learned an important lesson in the American Revolution. It later enacted special concessionary statutes, now often miscalled "constitutions" for certain of its "Dominions" including Canada and Australia. By this device it was able to keep the British Empire intact and thus escape the immediate necessity for bringing its authority to bear too directly or too obviously upon the inhabitants of the British mainland.

AFTERMATH OF WORLD WAR   With the all but complete collapse of the British Empire in World War II, the long deferred climax of the "glorious revolution" could be restrained no longer. There are few places now for the ruthless rigor of British Statism to manifest itself except upon the person and property of individual Englishmen. The present Socialist Government of England lost no time in promptly cancelling the time-honored paroles which some of its more naive subjects had come to regard as "English liberties." To end this confusion once and for all the Attorney General of Eng-

land, Sir Hartley Shawcross, M.P., in 1946 had to remind
the English people that:

> "Parliament is sovereign; it may make *any* laws. It
> could ordain that all blue-eyed babies be destroyed
> at birth."

But of course the Attorney-General was merely restating
the old absolutist doctrine against which Americans successfully rebelled in 1776. It was on the very eve of the
American Revolution that Blackstone wrote:

> "If the Parliament will positively enact a thing to be
> done which is unreasonable, I know of no power in
> the ordinary forms of the Constitution that is vested
> with authority to control it."

Where the power of government is incapable of restraint by the individual citizen in the orderly judicial
process of protecting his unalienable natural rights, no
subject of such a government is *free*. Consequently such
government does violence to the inherent nature of man.
It was precisely upon this principle of the Natural Law
that the American Revolution was fought and the independence of the American Republic accomplished.

TRUST IN The sensitivity of the average Englishman
BALLOT to the despotic nature of Parliamentary government was and is undoubtedly dulled by
the fact that the membership of the House of Commons
is periodically determined by general popular elections.
For many years the Englishmen's government has thus
been the creature of his ballot with the result that he

developed a confidence in Parliament that is sharply contrasted with the distrust and suspicion with which his ancestors regarded the English Kings.

It was precisely during this long period of suspicion and distrust that recognition of traditional English liberties was wrested from the crown and protected by a lengthy series of restrictions upon the Royal prerogatives. For these liberties the Englishmen paid the standard price of "Eternal Vigilance." From Magna Charta forward to the "glorious Revolution" of 1688, the *drive* of the English populace was toward a "voice" in their government and concurrent restrictions upon royal power which did not acknowledge the people as its source.

When the reins of government finally passed to the people's representatives in Parliament, popular vigilance relaxed. The ultimate result was a popular tolerance for Parliamentary measures, which, in the form of Royal decrees would have been the signal for a new battle of Runnymede.

EXTENT OF POWER THE ISSUE This unfortunate attitude toward "popular" government is a general one. It results from the widespread false impression that any government is safe and good so long as the people choose it themselves. The truth is that tyranny depends entirely upon the *extent* of governmental power and is in no way related to the *source* of that power.

A popularly elected tyranny is often more rapacious than a despot who takes his power by force or inheritance. For instance, the popularly elected Socialist government of England has withdrawn more privileges and immunities from great masses of Englishmen and imposed more compulsions upon them than any one of the most despotic English Kings would have dared to decree. Of course the Socialists did all that they have done with a professed dedication to the general welfare. Nevertheless, the motive does not diminish the area of the personal deprivations. Nor can it be expected, on the basis of the evidence of five thousand years of recorded history that the Socialist program has spent itself.

Unchecked Absolutism cannot rest with half-way measures. The rationale of its very existence demands

> the *full and complete subjection of every person and thing within its jurisdiction to the totality of its plans for the whole society.*

A new generation of Englishmen will reap the real harvest of this newly operating tyranny. It has thus been correctly stated that Socialism is Communism on a slow train. Socialism performs its totalitarian operations under the anesthetic of "democratic" terminology while Communism draws the same blood visibly, violently and with an open profession of its complete and unrestrained dictatorship.

ESCAPE THROUGH SOCIALISM Undoubtedly there are many sincere people who regard Socialism as a "democratic" institution which offers an escape from Communism rather than a retreat into its arms. There were many such people in Poland, Hungary, Rumania, Bulgaria and Czechoslovakia a few years ago, but at the present time those of them who are still alive all know better. After all, it was not necessary that these people should have had to learn this lesson the hard way. For instance, in 1936, Mr. John Strachey wrote in his "Theory and Practice of Socialism":

> "It is impossible to establish communism as the immediate successor to capitalism. It is, accordingly, proposed to establish socialism as something which we can put in the place of our present decaying capitalism. Hence, Communists work for the establishment of socialism as a necessary transition stage on the road of communism."

> At this writing, Mr. Strachey is War Minister in the Socialist government of Great Britain.

English experience was a lesson to America in 1776 and we certainly should take another lesson from England today. If the ballot box cannot defend personal rights in England you may be sure that voting alone will not protect personal rights in America.

The tyranny of a majority can be even more terrible than the tyranny of an individual despot. Personal despotisms are sometimes benevolent, but benevolence is never a characteristic of a mob. If we are ready to settle for unrestricted majority rule in America today we must prepare for even worse ordeals than those now being suffered by our English brethren in the land where Magna Charta is still officially revered, even tho its basic principle is no longer respected.

CHAPTER EIGHT

Our America

STATE ABSOLUTISM is no respecter of persons or places. It can and does raise its ugly, un-Godly standard over the traditionally free soil of England with the same brash assurance that characterizes its sway in the land of the Czars. Always and everywhere it is at war with the free, God-given nature of man. For that reason alone, none of the real, pretended or promised benefits of State absolutism can possibly justify its existence. It is out to destroy man and consequently man must destroy it in self defense.

This all-powerful State has definite designs upon the one place on earth where the formula for effective resistance to it was conceived, established and justified in practice. That one place is America. We have examined this American formula in specification and detail. At this point we need only to recall that the substance of the formula is

> *continuous, strict and closely guarded limitations upon the power of government.*

Neither the peril of war nor the promise of welfare must ever serve to relax any item of this formula unless we are prepared to subject ourselves to the perverted dehumanized condition of slavery.

VARIATIONS IN FORM   Despotism never advertises itself as such. Invariably it is a wolf in sheep's clothing. By its own definition it will be "democratic," "progressive," "liberal," "humanitarian" and "fraternal." Those who oppose it will be called reactionaries, fascists and other currently bad names. It is not by its name, therefore, that you shall know Absolutism, but by what it proposes to do. Whenever relaxation of existing limitations upon the power of government is suggested, you are upon notice that your liberty is threatened. Unless you counterattack swiftly and sharply you are likely to be denatured.

Proper vigilance against despotism is particularly difficult when the proponents of the all-powerful state deliberately appropriate the language of liberalism. Traditionally a liberal was a person who believed in the rights of man against government. Recently, however, the professed liberal is one who wishes in one way or another to *liberate government* from its natural and Constitutional limitations. This process of governmental liberation takes different forms at different times. In recent years the process has taken the form of taxing and spending by the Federal government. The successful use of this form of governmental liberation constitutes the most serious threat ever made against the maintenance of constitutional limitations in the United States.

UNLIMITED POWER   Unless constitutional limitations upon the spending powers of Congress are effectively and speedily established, all other constitutional limitations will soon be swept aside in our constantly accelerated drive toward centralized socialism. Money is power and, when the materialistic concept controls, unlimited money is unlimited power.

Today, big and complicated government has a hand in everybody's business and another in every person's pocket. These hands are moved by relatively obscure people tucked away here and there throughout the fathomless mazes of government's bulging burocracy. The brooding government omnipresence is an open invitation to those who wish to use one or more of government's complicated processes for unfair advantage over their neighbors. Strings are pulled, leaks of information are accomplished, investigations are launched, all to the irreparable damage of many people—but all according to law.

POWER BY SUBSIDY   It is useless to claim personal rights or "State's Rights" against a Federal government that is able to subsidize with unlimited money any form of local activity that it favors while it withholds such rewards from similar activities that fail to meet the required federal specifications. In the unchallenged exercise of its limitless power to spend and lend, Congress can buy its way into complete centralized control of such matters as health, education, insurance, agriculture, banking and manufacturing. It may subsidize newspapers and magazines with an obvious effect upon "Freedom" of the press. By an extension of the established practice of "grants-in-aid" to the States, it can and does reduce the time-honored exercise of State sovereignty to the role of local agent for the big Federal boss.

POLITICAL INCENTIVE Such procedures are good politics with candidates who are more interested in attaining office than they are in preserving the essentials of Americanism. To such candidates every election is an auction where federal appropriations are promised to the group with the greatest number of votes. "Ability to pay" is no longer a practical restraint upon Congressional spending. Our recent prolonged experience with wholesale deficit financing has shown an effective way for the Federal Government to spend what it does not have and that which *it never seriously expects to have*. The purpose of federal taxes now is only incidentally to raise necessary revenue. The principal purpose behind most forms of the many federal excises is to rearrange and control accumulations of private wealth and level the peaks and valleys of the social and economic terrain. This is not American freedom;

it is socialistic regimentation by a government that has shaken loose from its constitutional limitations.

In the face of such congressional omnipotence, the citizen of the United States may soon be reduced to the helpless political level of a British subject in Socialistic England. From that point, depression to the British economic level will only be a matter of time.

CURRENT CONCEPT How has American government thus managed to escape the powerful and strict constitutional limitations placed upon it by the Founding Fathers? The answer is found in the changed attitude of the American people. In recent years we have been educated to believe that the general welfare requires a strong centralized government with practically unlimited powers. Of course this attitude violates the logic of our own glorious history and ignores the tragic failures of centralized governments elsewhere in the world. Nevertheless, the present "scholarly" development of American Constitutional law has reached this conclusion:

> Law is what government does. If you don't like what the government does, you may write and talk against it and vote against it at the next election. Your speech, writing and vote must be free from governmental interference, but beyond that you are free to do only what government allows you to do.

The whole field of American liberty has thus been reduced to free speech and a free vote. To reach this absurd conclusion, the "scholars" have found it necessary to ridicule the "pious absolutes" of the Declaration of Independence while they pay a cheap lip service to the American constitutional system. The fact that they have

managed to give this conclusion an academic respect-
ability, demonstrates the dangerous power of Absolutism
when it wears a clever false face. It also demonstrates the
possibilities of popular education. This should give us
our cue.

**IMPERATIVE
NEED**
Ours is the task of re-educating the public
in the essentiality and desirability of maintaining and strengthening limitations upon
government in the interest of preserving necessary human
freedom. Remember that where government is unlimited
no citizen is free. All-powerful government is a working
synonym for tyranny. Our Forefathers knew this and
consequently they made *the limitation of government* the
controlling feature of the American Constitutional System.
Each section and each branch of government was made
into a limitation upon the other. This was certainly not
done in the interest of streamlined efficiency—quite the
contrary. It was done deliberately to slow down governmental action in the interest of the freedom and security
of the individual citizen. All human governments are
constantly and naturally striving for an increase of their
powers. This is rationalized by the "incentive impulse"
of politicians. American Government has been no excep-
tion. Constitutional limitations are consequently subject
to an ever-increasing strain upon their effectiveness.

**DEFENDERS OF
AMERICANISM**
It is not that "Americanism," so-called,
no longer has defenders—the mails, the
magazines, the radio and television

waves are all heavily freighted with arguments for "the American Way." However, the arguments always boil down to a defense of the American System in terms of Private Enterprise. The approach is that of an exhaustive statistical balance sheet of material assets and liabilities. They tell us that the "American System" must be preserved because:

> "We have more bathtubs here per square inch than Russia has per square mile; that we have practically all the private telephones and automobiles in the world together with the highest material standard of living ever attained by any people at any time in history."

Now all this is well and good, true enough and very important. But, the American System will never be saved through the pulling power of such evidence. If—God save the mark—we should ever lose these purely material advantages—then by the clear implication of all of these arguments the "American System" should be scrapped.

GIVE THEM THE BATHTUBS For the sake of argument we could stipulate away the bathtubs, the telephones, the automobiles, and the standard of living to the Russians or the Chinese and still prove that despite these material losses, the American Constitutional System will continue to be the most sublime pattern for human society that has ever been or can be devised. We did not have any of these material advantages in America in 1776, nevertheless the founders of our country readily risked their lives, fortunes and sacred honor for the legal establishment of what they knew was a *sound principle of eternal truth.*

The material things, the bathtubs, automobiles—the Standard of Living—these things are the *consequences* of the American System. They are conclusive evidence to show the workability and serviceability of the basic American principle which is the source and the cause of our comparative comfort and prosperity. That basic causative American Principle is the important consideration in the great debate and the principle is this:

> An uncompromising and uncompromised demand for the freedom and independence of the individual man. If the man is free and independent the material things will accrue to him and flow into his society as a matter of course.

That was the thesis of the Founding Fathers. It is the genius of our Constitutional System. That System is not the best merely because the great majority of our people love the institution of private property and fear and hate Communism. If the Communistic threat is to be liquidated, Communism must be defeated on *principle.* It will never be defeated by making those very social, economic and political concessions to Socialism which Karl Marx advocated as necessary prerequisites to the ultimate establishment of Communism itself.

TWO SHIRTS UNNECESSARY It isn't necessary for a man to have a job or a second shirt to his back before he can become devoted to and be depended upon to support the American principle of personal liberty although such a man should and probably would have both. The love of and necessity for personal liberty is a part of each man's God-given nature. It is a birthright which only the grossly misinformed will sell for a mess of materialistic pottage.

ALL PRECEDENTS DEFIED In instituting the system of firmly and expressly limited government, the Founding Fathers defied all the precedents of history and committed a positive affront to the persistent and perennial ruler of men—*Despotism*. They knew that every government is by its nature an incipient tyranny and that no number of Constitutional chains can effectively restrain it where the people are not continuously alert to the all important necessity for its continued restraint.

In threatening America, despotism threatens all humanity everywhere in the world. Today the fate of civilization depends upon the sustained strengthened solvency of all that is implied in the expression "The United States of America." If our power should suddenly disintegrate the whole human race soon would be enveloped in a fog of terror so demoralizing and so devastating that those who momentarily survived it would envy those who did not.

While we stand firm all human nature hopes and prays for ultimate deliverance. Our firmness is in our God-given freedom and our freedom is in our successful resistance to all-powerful government.

STORY MUST BE TOLD This is the story that needs to be amplified around the world—into the ears of hungry, depressed and oppressed Poles, Yugoslavs, Italians, Czechs, Rumanians, Greeks, Frenchmen, Bulgarians, Chinese and particularly the Russians. This is the saga of man's spirit released from the satanic bondage of political materialism. This is the *substance* of Americanism. A bloody revolution was necessary to establish it. A desperate civil war was necessary to maintain it. May God grant that the time may never come but, if it becomes essential, other wars must be fought to preserve and perpetuate this exclusive and priceless heritage for it is—the Key to Peace.

Our One World Planners must be made to remember that the famine-stricken populations of the old world cannot live now or hereafter by bread alone, nor indeed can we. Those in charge of our national defense must be made to realize that if the fascinating American story is made plain to our actual and potential enemies military opposition will liquidate itself in the wild scramble to follow the American example.

All over the world there is an immediate demand for enormous quantities of pure Americanism, but unfortunately, the demand comes at a time when we are experiencing a critical shortage right here in the United

States. In order to have an exportable surplus of this priceless product, we must intensify and multiply its production in America. Like Charity, which it so much resembles, Americanism begins at home. You and I must know and understand these vital principles before we can explain and export them to others.

In the presently prevailing fog of misunderstanding, the task of propagating American principles will not be an easy one. We shall meet militant resistance at every stage of the struggle. To win, we must remember that our battle is not against any people or any system. Primarily it is neither military nor economic. The battle is spiritual, and it is waged against despotism. Our ramparts are behind the deathless and self-evident truths of The Declaration of Independence.

"Remove not the ancient Landmark which thy fathers have set."

EPILOGUE

The need now is not for "new concepts," "fresh approaches" and "ingenious improvisations" in the cause of peace and unity. The need now is for rediscovery, and renewed understanding of the true and tried principle of Americanism. In the strange and striking record of our own country this precious gem of human understanding lies buried. Let us dig here and now for the subtle secret of 1776.

While civilization exhausts itself in fruitless searches all over the world, it would be tragic indeed if this simple yet entirely effective formula for the complete peace and happiness of humanity is permitted to lie unheeded in the unturned pages of American History.

The diamond mines of Golconda were discovered in Hafed's backyard.

APPENDIX

The United States Supreme Court has ruled that,—
"THIS IS A RELIGIOUS NATION".

A digest of this vital decision immediately follows.

"This Is A Religious Nation"

Digest of Supreme Court Decision

The Rector, Church Wardens, and Vestrymen of
THE CHURCH OF THE HOLY TRINITY, Plffs. in Err.

v.

UNITED STATES*

Mr. Justice Brewer delivered the opinion of the court:

Plaintiff in error is a corporation duly organized and incorporated as a religious society under the laws of the state of New York. E. Walpole Warren was, prior to September, 1887, an alien residing in England. In that month the plaintiff in error made a contract with him, by which he was to remove to the city of New York, and enter into its service as rector and pastor; and, in pursuance of such contract, Warren did so remove and enter upon such service. It is claimed by the United States that this contract on the part of the plaintiff in error was forbidden by chapter 164, 23 St. p. 332; and an action was commenced to recover the penalty prescribed by that act. The circuit court held that the contract was within the prohibition of the statute, and rendered judgment accordingly, (36 Fed. Rep. 303,) and the single question presented for our determination is whether it erred in that conclusion.

The first section describes the act forbidden, and is in these words:

> "Be it enacted by the Senate and House of Representatives of the United States of America, in Congress assembled, that from and after the passage of this Act it shall be unlawful for any person, company, partnership, or corporation, in any manner whatsoever, to prepay the transportation, or in any way assist or encourage the importation or migration, of any alien or aliens, any foreigner or foreigners, into the United States, its territories, or the District of Columbia, under contract or agreement, parol or special, express or implied, made previous to the importation or migration of such alien or aliens, foreigner or foreigners, to perform labor or service of any kind in the United States, its territories, or the District of Columbia."

It must be conceded that the act of the corporation is within the letter of this section, for the relation of rector to his church is one of service, and implies labor on the one side with compensation on the other. Not only are the general words "labor" and "service" both used, but also, as it were to guard against any narrow inter-

*(1892, 143 U. S. 457)

pretation and emphasize a breadth of meaning, to them is added "of any kind"; and, further, as noticed by the circuit judge in his opinion, the fifth section, which makes specific exceptions, among them professional actors, artists, lecturers, singers, and domestic servants, strengthens the idea that every other kind of labor and service was intended to be reached by the first section. While there is great force to this reasoning, we cannot think Congress intended to denounce with penalties a transaction like that in the present case. (The discussion of the meaning of the title of the act, the evil to be remedied, the letter and the spirit of the statute and the circumstances surrounding its passage by Congress is omitted.)

But, beyond all these matters, no purpose of action against religion can be imputed to any legislation, state or national, because this is a religious people. This is historically true. From the discovery of this continent to the present hour, there is a single voice making this affirmation.

The commission to Christopher Columbus, prior to his sail westward, is from

> "Ferdinand and Isabella, by the grace of God, King and Queen of Castile," etc.,

and recites that

> "it is hoped that by God's assistance some of the continents and islands in the ocean will be discovered," etc.

The first colonial grant, that made to Sir Walter Raleigh in 1584 was from

> "Elizabeth, by the grace of God, of England, Frunce and Ireland, queene, defender of the faith," etc.;

and the grant authorizing him to enact statutes of the government of the proposed colony provided that,—

> "they be not against the true Christian faith nowe professed in the Church of England."

The first charter of Virginia, granted by King James I in 1606, after reciting the application of certain parties for a charter, commenced the grant in these words:

> "We, greatly commending, and graciously accepting of, their Desires for the Furtherance of so noble a Work, which may, by the Providence of Almighty God, hereafter tend to the Glory of his Divine Majesty, in propagating of Christian Religion to such People, as yet live in Darkness and miserable Ignorance of the true Knowledge and Worship of God, and may in time bring the Infidels and Savages, living in those parts, to human Civility, and to a settled and quiet Government; DO, by these our Letters-Patents, graciously accept of, and agree to, their humble and well-intended Desires."

Language of similar import may be found in the subsequent charters of that colony, from the same king, in 1609 and 1611; and the same is true of the various charters granted to the other colonies. In language more or less emphatic is the establishment of the Christian religion declared to be one of the purposes of the grant. The celebrated compact made by the Pilgrims in the Mayflower, 1620, recites:

> "Having undertaken for the Glory of God, and Advancement of the Christian Faith, and the Honour of our King and Country, a Voyage to plant the first Colony in the northern Parts of Virginia; Do by these Presents, solemnly and mutually, in the Presence of God and one another, covenant and combine ourselves together into a civil Body Politick, for our better Ordering and Preservation, and Furtherance of the Ends aforesaid."

The fundamental orders of Connecticut, under which a provisional government was instituted in 1638-39, commence with this declaration:

> "Forasmuch as it hath pleased the Allmighty God by the wise disposition of his diuyne pruidence so to Order and dispose of things that we the Inhabitants and Residents of Windsor, Hartford, and Wethersfield are now cohabiting and dwelling in and vppon the River of Conectecotte and the Lands thereunto adioyneing; And well knowing where a people are gathered togather the word of God requires that to mayntayne the peace and vnion of such a people their should be an orderly and decent Gouerment established according to God, to order and dispose of the affayres of the people at all seasons as occation shall require; doe therefor assotiate and conioyne our selues to be as one Publike like State or Comonwelth; and doe, for our selues and our Successors and such as shall be adioyned to vs att any tyme hereafter, enter into Combination and Confederation togather, to mayntayne and presearue the liberty and purity of the gospell of our Lord Jesus wch we now prfesse, as also the disciplyne of the Churches, wch according to the truth of the said gospell is now practised amongst vs."

In the charter of privileges granted by William Penn to the province of Pennsylvania, in 1701, it is recited:

> "Because no People can be truly happy, though under the greatest Enjoyment of Civil Liberties, if abridged of the Freedom of their Consciences, as to their Religious Profession and Worship; And Almighty God being the only Lord of Conscience, Father of Lights and Spirits; and the Author as well as Object of all divine Knowledge, Faith, and Worship, who only doth enlighten the Minds, and persuade and convince the Understandings of People, I do hereby grant and declare," etc.

Coming nearer to the present time, the Declaration of Independence recognizes the presence of the Divine in human affairs in these words:

> "We hold these truths to be self evident, that all men are created equal, that they are endowed by their Creator with certain unalienable Rights,

that among these are Life, Liberty, and the pursuit of Happiness." "We, therefore, the Representatives of the united States of America, in General Congress, Assembled, appealing to the Supreme Judge of the world for the rectitude of our intentions, do, in the Name and by Authority of the good People of these Colonies, solemnly publish and declare," etc.; "And for the support of this Declaration, with a firm reliance on the Protection of Divine Providence, we mutually pledge to each other and our Lives, our Fortunes, and our sacred Honor."

If we examine the constitutions of the various states, we find in them a constant recognition of religious obligations. Every constitution of every one of the forty-four states contains language which, either directly or by clear implication, recognizes a profound reverence for religion, and an assumption that its influence in all human affairs is essential to the well-being of the community. This recognition may be in the preamble, such as is found in the constitution of Illinois, 1870:

> "We, the people of the state of Illinois, grateful to Almighty God for the civil, political, and religious liberty which He hath so long permitted us to enjoy, and looking to Him for a blessing upon our endeavors to secure and transmit the same unimpaired to succeeding generations," etc.

It may be only in the familiar requisition that all officers shall take an oath closing with the declaration, "so help me God." It may be in clauses like that of the constitution of Indiana, 1816, art. XI, section 4:

> "The manner of administering an oath or affirmation shall be such as is most consistent with the conscience of the deponent, and shall be esteemed the most solemn appeal to God."

Or in provisions such as are found in articles 36 and 37 of the declaration of rights of the constitution of Maryland, (1867:)

> "That, as it is the duty of every man to worship God in such manner as he thinks most acceptable to Him, all persons are equally entitled to protection in their religious liberty: wherefore, no person ought, by any law, to be molested in his person or estate on account of his religious persuasion or profession, or for his religious practice, unless, under the color of religion, he shall disturb the good order, peace, or safety of the state, or shall infringe the laws of morality, or injure others in their natural, civil, or religious rights; nor ought any person to be compelled to frequent or maintain or contribute, unless on contract, to maintain any place of worship or any ministry; nor shall any person, otherwise competent, be deemed incompetent as a witness or juror on account of his religious belief: provided, he believes in the existence of God, and that, under his dispensation, such person will be held morally accountable for his acts, and be rewarded or punished therefor, either in this world or the world to come. That no religious test ought ever to be required as a qualification for any office of profit or trust in this state, other than a declaration of belief in the existence of

God; nor shall the legislature prescribe any other oath of office than the oath prescribed by this constitution."

Or like that in articles 2 and 3, of part 1 of the constitution of Massachusetts, (1780:)

"It is the right as well as the duty of all men in society publicly, and at stated seasons, to worship the Supreme Being, the great Creator and Preserver of the universe: . . . As the happiness of a people and the good order and preservation of civil government essentially depend upon piety, religion, and morality, and as these cannot be generally diffused through a community but by the institution of the public worship of God and of public instructions in piety, religion, and morality: Therefore, to promote their happiness, and to secure the good order and preservation of their government, the people of this commonwealth have a right to invest their legislature with power to authorize and require, and the legislature shall, from time to time, authorize and require, the several towns, parishes, precincts, and other bodies politic or religious societies to make suitable provision, at their own expense, for the institution of the public worship of God and for the support and maintenance of public Protestant teachers of piety, religion, and morality, in all cases where such provision shall not be made voluntarily."

Or, as in sections 5 and 14 of article 7 of the constitution of Mississippi, (1832:)

"No person who denies the being of a God, or a future state of rewards and punishments, shall hold any office in the civil department of this state......Religion, morality, and knowledge being necessary to good government, the preservation of liberty, and the happiness of mankind, schools, and the means of education, shall forever be encouraged in this state."   . . . . . .

Or by article 22 of the constitution of Delaware, (1776,) which required all officers, besides an oath of allegiance, to make and subscribe the following declaration:

"I, A.B., do profess faith in God the Father, and in Jesus Christ His only Son, and in the Holy Ghost, one God, blessed for evermore; and I do acknowledge the Holy Scriptures of the Old and New Testament to be given by divine inspiration."

Even the constitution of the United States, which is supposed to have little touch upon the private life of the individual, contains in the 1st amendment a declaration common to the constitutions of all the states, as follows:

"Congress shall make no law respecting an establishment of religion, or prohibiting the free exercise thereof," etc.,—

and also provides in article I, section 7, (a provision common to many constitutions,) that the executive shall have ten days (Sundays excepted) within which to determine whether he will approve or veto a bill.

There is no dissonance in these declarations. There is a universal language pervading them all, having one meaning. They affirm and reaffirm that this is a religious nation. These are not individual sayings, declarations of private persons. They are organic utterances. They speak the voice of the entire people. While because of a general recognition of this truth the question has seldom been presented to the courts, yet we find that in Updegraph v. Com., 11 Serg. & R. 394, 400, it was decided that,

> "Christianity, general Christianity, is, and always has been, a part of the common law of Pennsylvania; . . . not Christianity with an established church and tithes and spiritual courts, but Christianity with liberty of conscience to all men."

And in People v. Ruggles, 8 Johns. 290, 294, 295, Chancellor Kent, the great commentator on American law, speaking as chief justice of the supreme court of New York, said:

> "The people of this state, in common with the people of this country, profess the general doctrines of Christianity as the rule of their faith and practice; and to scandalize the author of these doctrines is not only, in a religious point of view, extremely impious, but, even in respect to the obligations due to society, is a gross violation of decency, and good order. . . . The free, equal, and undisturbed enjoyment of religious opinion, whatever it may be, and free and decent discussions on any religious subject, is granted and secured; but to revile, with malicious and blasphemous contempt, the religion professed by almost the whole community is an abuse of that right. Nor are we bound by any expressions in the constitution, as some have strangely supposed, either not to punish at all, or to punish indiscriminately the like attacks upon the religion of Mahomet or of the Grand Lama; and for this plain reason, that the case assumes that we are a Christian people, and the morality of the country is deeply ingrafted upon Christianity, and not upon the doctrines or worship of imposters."

And in the famous case of Vidal v. Girard's Ex'rs, 2 How. 127, 198, this court, while sustaining the will of Mr. Girard, with its provision for the creation of a college into which no minister shall be permitted to enter, observed:

> "It is also said, and truly, that the Christian religion is a part of the common law of Pennsylvania."

If we pass beyond these matters to a view of American life, as expressed by its laws, its business, its customs, and its society, we find everywhere a clear recognition of the same truth. Among other matters note the following:

> The form of oath universally prevailing, concluding with an appeal to the Almighty; the custom of opening sessions of all deliberative bodies and most conventions with prayer; the prefatory words of all

wills, "In the name of God, amen;" the laws respecting the observance of the Sabbath, with the general cessation of all secular business, and the closing of courts, legislatures, and other similar public assemblies on that day; the churches and church organizations which abound in every city, town, and hamlet; the multitude of charitable organizations existing everywhere under Christian auspices; the gigantic missionary associations, with general support, and aiming to establish Christian missions in every quarter of the globe.

These, and many other matters which might be noticed, add a volume of unofficial declarations to the mass of organic utterances that this is a Christian nation.

In the face of all these, shall it be believed that a congress of the United States intended to make it a misdemeanor for a church of this country to contract for the services of a Christian minister residing in another nation?

Suppose, in the congress that passed this Act, some member had offered a bill which in terms declared that, if any Roman Catholic church in this country should contract with Cardinal Manning to come to this country, and enter into its service as pastor and priest, or any Episcopal church should enter into a like contract with Canon Farrar, or any Baptist church should make similar arrangements with Rev. Mr. Spurgeon, or any Jewish synagogue with some eminent rabbi, such contract should be adjudged unlawful and void, and the church making it be subject to prosecution and punishment. Can it be believed that it would have received a minute of approving thought or a single vote? Yet it is contended that such was, in effect, the meaning of this statute. The construction invoked cannot be accepted as correct.

It is a case where there was presented a definite evil, in view of which the legislature used general terms with the purpose of reaching all phases of that evil; and thereafter, unexpectedly, it is developed that the general language thus employed is broad enough to reach cases and acts which the whole history and life of the country affirm could not have been intentionally legislated against. It is the duty of the courts, under those circumstances, to say that, however broad the language of the statute may be, the act, although within the letter, is not within the intention of the legislature, and therefore cannot be within the statute.

The judgment will be reversed, and the case remanded for further proceedings in accordance with this opinion.

Excerpts from Preambles of Forty-seven State Constitutions and Dates of Adoption

ALABAMA 1901

We, the people of the State of Alabama, in order to establish justice, insure domestic tranquillity and secure the blessings of liberty to ourselves and our posterity, invoking the favor and guidance of Almighty God, do ordain and establish the following Constitution and form of government for the State of Alabama.

ARIZONA 1912

We, the people of the State of Arizona, grateful to Almighty God for our liberties, do ordain this Constitution.

ARKANSAS 1874

We, the people of the State of Arkansas, grateful to Almighty God for the privilege of choosing our own form of government, for our civil and religious liberty, and desiring to perpetuate its blessings and secure the same to ourselves and posterity, do ordain and establish this Constitution.

CALIFORNIA 1879

We, the people of the State of California, grateful to Almighty God for our freedom, in order to secure and perpetuate its blessings, do establish this Constitution.

COLORADO 1876

We, the people of Colorado, with profound reverence for the Supreme Ruler of the Universe, in order to form a more independent and perfect government; establish justice; insure tranquillity; provide for the common defense; promote the general welfare and secure the blessings of liberty to ourselves and our posterity; do ordain and establish this Constitution for the "State of Colorado."

CONNECTICUT 1818

The people of Connecticut acknowledging with gratitude, the good providence of God, in having permitted them to enjoy a free government, do, in order more effectually to define, secure, and perpetuate the liberties, rights and privileges which they have derived from their ancestors, hereby, after a careful consideration and revision, ordain and establish the following Constitution and form of civil government.

DELAWARE 1897

Through Divine goodness, all men have by nature the rights of worshipping and serving their Creator according to the dictates of their consciences, of enjoying and defending life and liberty, of acquiring and protecting reputation and property, and in general of obtaining objects suitable to their condition, without injury by one to another; and as these rights are essential to their welfare, for the due exercise thereof, power is inherent in them; and therefore all just authority in the institutions of political society is derived from the people, and established with their consent, to advance their happiness; and they may for this end, as circumstances require, from time to time alter their Constitution of government.

116

FLORIDA 1887

We, the people of the State of Florida, grateful to Almighty God for our constitutional liberty, in order to secure its blessings and to form a more perfect government, insuring domestic tranquillity, maintaining public order, and guaranteeing equal civil and political rights to all, do ordain and establish this Constitution.

GEORGIA 1887

To perpetuate the principles of free government, insure justice to all, preserve peace, promote the interest and happiness of the citizen, and transmit to posterity the enjoyment of liberty, we, the people of Georgia, relying upon the protection and guidance of Almighty God, do ordain and establish this Constitution.

IDAHO 1890

We, the people of the State of Idaho, grateful to Almighty God for our freedom, to secure its blessings and promote our common welfare, do establish this Constitution.

ILLINOIS 1870

We, the people of the State of Illinois—grateful to Almighty God for the civil, political and religious liberty which He hath so long permitted us to enjoy, and looking to Him for a blessing upon our endeavors to secure and transmit the same unimpaired to succeeding generations—in order to form a more perfect government, establish justice, insure domestic tranquillity, provide for the common defense, promote the general welfare, and secure the blessing of liberty to ourselves and our posterity, do ordain and establish this Constitution for the State of Illinois.

INDIANA 1851

To the end that justice be established, public order maintained, and liberty perpetuated: We, the people of the State of Indiana, grateful to Almighty God for the free exercise of the right to choose our own form of government, do ordain this Constitution.

IOWA 1857

We, the people of the State of Iowa, grateful to the Supreme Being for the blessings hitherto enjoyed, and feeling our dependence on Him for a continuation of those blessings, do ordain and establish a free and independent government, by the name of the State of Iowa, the boundaries whereof shall be as follows:

KANSAS 1863

We, the people of Kansas, grateful to Almighty God for our civil and religious privileges, in order to insure the full enjoyment of our rights as American citizens, do ordain and establish this Constitution of the State of Kansas, with the following boundaries, to wit: Beginning at a point on the western boundary of the State of Missouri, where the thirty-seventh parallel of north latitude crosses the same; thence running west on said parallel to the twenty-fifth meridian of longitude west from Washington; thence north on said meridian to the fortieth parallel of north latitude; thence east on said parallel to the western boundary of the State of Missouri, thence south with the western boundary of said state to the place of beginning.

KENTUCKY 1891

We, the people of the Commonwealth of Kentucky, grateful to Almighty God for the civil, political and religious liberties we enjoy, and invoking the continuance of these blessings, do ordain and establish this Constitution.

LOUISIANA 1921

We, the people of the State of Louisiana, grateful to Almighty God for the civil, political and religious liberties we enjoy, and desiring to secure the continuance of these blessings, do ordain and establish this Constitution.

MAINE 1820 and 1876

We, the people of Maine, in order to establish justice, insure tranquillity, provide for our mutual defense, promote our common welfare, and secure to ourselves and our posterity the blessings of liberty, acknowledging with grateful hearts the goodness of the Sovereign Ruler of the Universe in affording us an opportunity, so favorable to the design; and, imploring His aid and direction in its accomplishment, do agree to form ourselves into a free and independent State, by the style and title of the State of Maine, and do ordain and establish the following Constitution for the government of the same.

MARYLAND 1867

We, the people of the State of Maryland, grateful to Almighty God for our civil and religious liberty, and taking into our serious consideration the best means of establishing a good Constitution in this State for the sure foundation and more permanent security thereof, declare:

MASSACHUSETTS 1790

We, therefore, the people of Massachusetts, acknowledging, with grateful hearts, the goodness of the great Legislator of the universe, in affording us, in the course of His providence, an opportunity, deliberately and peaceably, without fraud, violence, or surprise, of entering into an original, explicit, and solemn compact with each other; and for forming a new Constitution of civil government, for ourselves and posterity; and devoutly imploring His direction in so interesting a design, do agree upon, ordain, and establish the following Declaration of Rights, and Frame of Government, as the Constitution of the Commonwealth of Massachusetts.

MICHIGAN 1909

We, the people of the State of Michigan, grateful to Almighty God for the blessings of freedom, and earnestly desiring to secure these blessings undiminished to ourselves and our posterity, do ordain and establish this Constitution.

MINNESOTA 1857

We, the people of the State of Minnesota, grateful to God for our civil and religious liberty and desiring to perpetuate its blessings and secure the same to ourselves and our posterity, do ordain and establish this Constitution.

MISSISSIPPI 1890

We, the people of Mississippi in convention assembled, grateful to Almighty God, and invoking his blessing on our work, do ordain and establish this Constitution.

MISSOURI 1945

We, the people of Missouri, with profound reverence for the Supreme Ruler of the Universe, and grateful for His goodness, do establish this Constitution for the better government of the State.

MONTANA 1889

We, the people of Montana, grateful to Almighty God for the blessings of liberty, in order to secure the advantages of a State government, do in accordance with the provisions of the enabling act of Congress, approve the twenty-second of February A. D. 1889, ordain and establish this Constitution.

NEBRASKA 1875

We, the people, grateful to Almighty God for our freedom, do ordain and establish the following declaration of rights and frame of government, as the Constitution of the State of Nebraska.

NEVADA 1864

We, the people of the State of Nevada, grateful to Almighty God for our freedom, in order to secure its blessings, insure domestic tranquillity, and form a more perfect government, do establish this Constitution.

NEW HAMPSHIRE 1784

Every individual has a natural and unalienable right to worship God according to the dictates of his own conscience, and reason * * * morality and piety, rightly grounded on evangelical principles, will give the best and greatest security to government, and will lay, in the hearts of men, the strongest obligations to due subjection; and the knowledge of these is most likely to be propagated through society by the institution of the public worship of the Deity.

NEW JERSEY 1947

We, the people of the State of New Jersey, grateful to Almighty God for the civil and religious liberty which He hath so long permitted us to enjoy, and looking to Him for a blessing upon our endeavors to secure and transmit the same unimpaired to succeeding generations, do ordain and establish this Constitution.

NEW MEXICO 1912

We, the people of New Mexico, grateful to Almighty God for the blessings of liberty, in order to secure the advantages of a State government, do ordain and establish this Constitution.

NEW YORK 1895

We, the people of the State of New York, grateful to Almighty God for our freedom, in order to secure its blessings, do establish this Constitution.

NORTH CAROLINA 1876

We, the people of the State of North Carolina, grateful to Almighty God, the Sovereign Ruler of Nations, for the preservation of the American Union and the existence of our civil, political and religious liberties, and acknowledging our dependence upon Him for the continuance of these blessings to us and our posterity, do, for the more certain security thereof and for the better government of this State, ordain and establish this Constitution.

NORTH DAKOTA 1889

We, the people of North Dakota, grateful to Almighty God for the blessings of civil and religious liberty, do ordain and establish this Constitution.

OHIO 1851

We, the people of the State of Ohio, grateful to Almighty God for our freedom, to secure its blessings and promote our common welfare, do establish this Constitution.

OKLAHOMA 1907

Invoking the guidance of Almighty God, in order to secure and perpetuate the blessing of liberty; to secure just and rightful government; to promote our mutual welfare and happiness, we the people of the State of Oklahoma, do ordain and establish this Constitution.

OREGON 1859

We, the people of the State of Oregon, to the end that justice be established, order maintained, and liberty perpetuated, do ordain this Constitution.

PENNSYLVANIA 1874

We, the people of the Commonwealth of Pennsylvania, grateful to Almighty God for the blessings of civil and religious liberty, and humbly invoking His guidance, do ordain and establish this Constitution.

RHODE ISLAND 1843

We, the people of the State of Rhode Island and Providence Plantations, grateful to Almighty God for the civil and religious liberty which He hath so long permitted us to enjoy, and looking to Him for a blessing upon our endeavors to secure and to transmit the same unimpaired to succeeding generations do ordain and establish this Constitution of Government.

SOUTH CAROLINA 1895

We, the people of the State of South Carolina, in convention assembled, grateful to God for our liberties, do ordain and establish this Constitution for the preservation and perpetuation of the same.

SOUTH DAKOTA 1889

We, the people of South Dakota, grateful to Almighty God for our civil and religious liberties, in order to form a more perfect and independent government, establish justice, insure tranquillity, provide for the common defense, promote the general welfare and preserve to ourselves and to our posterity the blessings of liberty, do ordain and establish this Constitution for the State of South Dakota.

TENNESSEE 1870

That all men have a natural and indefeasible right to worship Almighty God according to the dictates of their own conscience; that no man can of right, be compelled to attend, erect, or support any place of worship, or to maintain any minister against his consent; that no human authority can, in any case whatever, control or interfere with the rights of conscience; and that no preference shall ever be given, by law, to any religious establishment or mode of worship.

TEXAS 1876

Humbly invoking the blessings of Almighty God, the people of the State of Texas, do ordain and establish this Constitution.

UTAH 1895

Grateful to Almighty God for life and liberty, we, the people of Utah, in order to secure and perpetuate the principles of free government, do ordain and establish this Constitution.

VERMONT 1793

That all men have a natural and unalienable right, to worship Almighty God, according to the dictates of their own consciences and understandings, as in their opinion shall be regulated by the word of God: and that no man ought to or of right can be compelled to attend any religious worship, or erect or support any place of worship, or maintain any minister, contrary to the dictates of his conscience, nor can any man be justly deprived or abridged of any civil right as a citizen, on account of his religious sentiments, or peculiar mode of religious worship; and that no authority can, or ought to be vested in, or assumed by, any power whatever, that shall in any case interfere with, or in any manner control the rights of conscience, in the free exercise of religious worship. Nevertheless, every sect or denomination of christians ought to observe the sabbath or Lord's day, and keep up some sort of religious worship, which to them shall seem most agreeable to the revealed will of God.

VIRGINIA 1902

That religion or the duty which we owe to our Creator, and the manner of discharging it, can be directed only by reason and conviction, not by force or violence; and, therefore, all men are equally entitled to the free exercise of religion, according to the dictates of conscience; and that it is the mutual duty of all to practice Christian forbearance, love and charity towards each other.

WASHINGTON 1889

We, the people of the State of Washington, grateful to the Supreme Ruler of the Universe for our liberties, do ordain this Constitution.

WISCONSIN 1848

We, the people of Wisconsin, grateful to Almighty God for our freedom, in order to secure its blessings, form a more perfect government, insure domestic tranquillity and promote the general welfare, do establish this Constitution.

WYOMING 1889

We, the people of the State of Wyoming, grateful to God for our civil, political and religious liberties, and desiring to secure them to ourselves and perpetuate them to our posterity, do ordain and establish this Constitution.